C000144771

URBAN AND REGIONAL PLANNING IN JAMAICA

Pauline McHardy

UPFRONT PUBLISHING
LEICESTERSHIRE

ISBN 1 84426 019 4

First Published 2002 by
MINERVA PRESS

Second Edition 2002 by
UPFRONT PUBLISHING
Leicestershire

URBAN AND REGIONAL
PLANNING IN JAMAICA

Acknowledgements

My thanks go to the following for the use of illustrations as listed below:

Figure 2.4	Base Map Courtesy of the Director of Surveys, 23½ Charles Street, Kingston
Figure 2.10	West Indies Home Contractors, 27 Harbour Street, Kingston
Figure 3.1	Town Planning Department, 16 Oxford Road, Kingston
Figure 4.10	Kingston Restoration Company Limited, 3 Duke Street, Kingston
Figure 4.12	Town Planning Department, Kingston
Figure 4.15	Urban Development Corporation, 12 Ocean Boulevard, Kingston
Figure 4.16	Urban Development Corporation, Kingston
Figure 4.18	Town Planning Department, Kingston
Figure 4.21	Town Planning Department, Kingston
Figure 4.22	Urban Development Corporation, Kingston
Figure 4.23	Urban Development Corporation, Kingston
Figure 5.1	Town Planning Department, Kingston
Figure 5.2	Town Planning Department, Kingston
Figure 5.3	Town Planning Department, Kingston
Figure 5.4	Town Planning Department, Kingston
Figure 5.5	Town Planning Department, Kingston
Figure 5.6	Town Planning Department, Kingston
Figure 6.1	Town Planning Department, Kingston
Figure 6.4	Town Planning Department, Kingston

I also acknowledge permission granted by the following persons and organisations to use extracts from their works: G Thomas Kingsley of the Urban Institute, Washington DC and the Town Planning Department, Kingston.

About the Author

Pauline McHardy is a Jamaican. She received a BA degree in Geography and an MA degree in Community and Regional Planning from the University of British Columbia, Vancouver, Canada. She has considerable experience in urban and regional planning and human settlements development, having worked for the Government of Jamaica, the United Nations Development Programme (UNDP), and as a consultant to a number of regional and international agencies. She was the Chief Technical Advisor for the UNDP/UNCHS project, 'Institutional Development, Training and Operational Studies for the Shelter Sector' (Ghana, 1990–93). She is the author of a number of articles in the fields of planning, human settlements development and local government reform.

Preface

The idea for this book came as a result of the recognition of the paucity of material that exists on planning in developing countries such as Jamaica. Requests from practitioners and students for papers written by the author made it clear that there was a need for a book which evaluates the planning mechanisms and systems of countries which are newly independent. Jamaica, like many of these countries, adopted the planning systems of their former colonial masters. Hence, the need for a book which reviews planning practice and its response to the new and challenging demands on planning as we enter the twenty-first century.

This book is not intended to be a textbook on urban and regional planning, but is designed to provide new information on the subject which is not readily available elsewhere. In this regard therefore, the book hopes to add a new perspective – from the point of view of the developing world – and provide practitioners and students with an insight into the need for shifting paradigms. For those who want a traditional text on planning, they are urged to read J B McLoughlin's *Urban and Regional Planning: A Systems Approach* and F Stuart Chapin's *Urban Land Use Planning*. In addition, for those interested in the basic issues in the field of urban policy in developing countries, the following are recommended: *Taming the Megalopolis: A Design for Urban Growth* by Lauchlin Currie, *Cities in the Developing World: Policies for their Equitable and Efficient Growth* by Johannes F Linn and *Cities, Poverty and Development: Urbanisation in the Third World* by Gilbert and Gugler.

The book falls into four parts. Chapters I, II and III outline the development of the planning system in Jamaica. Chapter I outlines the concept and scope of planning in Jamaica and the problems associated with its definition while Chapter II traces the early history of planning in Jamaica. Chapter III analyses the setting up of the planning system and the effectiveness of policy instruments in protecting the urban and natural environment. Chapter IV discusses the process of urban change brought about by planned and unplanned urban development and redevelopment. Chapters V and VI review shifts in early paradigms and the introduction of new interpretations of what planning should be. Chapter V looks at national physical plans and attempts at improving links between economic and spatial planning. Chapter VI discusses the experience of regional planning and efforts made to bring about 'balanced regional development' through a national settlement strategy. Chapter VII outlines the effects of rapid urban growth and evaluates current paradigms in meeting the requirements of the expanding role of planning.

Glossary

Barber Greene: Type of asphalt road finish.

CBO: Community Based Organisation.

Digiport Centre: Facilities for information technology (IT) development.

Fee Simple: An estate of inheritance belonging to the owner, and transmissible to his heirs, absolutely and simply, without condition to the tenure.

LGRP: Local Government Reform Programme.

TIP: Tax Incentive Programme.

KMA: The Kingston Metropolitan Area is defined as the urban parts of the parish of St Andrew and the parish of Kingston, all of which is urban.

KSAC: In 1923 the parishes of Kingston and St Andrew were amalgamated into a single local authority, the Kingston and St Andrew Corporation (KSAC).

Quadraminium: Studio of a 12' by 18' room with a kitchen and bathroom. The units are constructed in clusters of four each and have two adjacent sides free standing to allow expansion.

Contents

List of Figures

Those Figures marked with ★ are situated in the photosection.

List of Tables

Chapter I

CONCEPTUAL FRAMEWORK OF PLANNING IN JAMAICA

Urban and regional planning has become well established as an integral part of the planning machinery of the country. The establishment of technology and degree courses at the University of Technology in the 1970s and 1980s and Masters programmes at the University of the West Indies in the 1990s provide credence to the growing importance of the discipline. However, despite the seemingly growing importance of planning and the introduction of statutory town planning forty-two years ago, the living conditions of a large proportion of the population in urban and rural settlements is still a major problem. These issues will be discussed in much greater detail in the ensuing chapters of the book.

While this book is not intended to be a textbook on urban and regional planning, a great deal of confusion exists in Jamaica regarding the concept and scope of planning. It is important therefore, that before we discuss the urban and regional planning process in Jamaica we should examine the problem of defining it. In this regard, it should be noted that urban and regional planning as we know it today has had a long history having evolved since the late nineteenth century. There is no space in this book to discuss the evolution of planning, therefore those who need to understand the development of planning ideas and policies, particularly students, should refer to the following: Cherry (1974), Faludi (1976, 1978), Hall (1988, 1992) and Ward (1994).

Defining Planning in Jamaica

Despite the fact that urban and regional planning was introduced as a discipline in Jamaica in 1947 there is still no clear notion of its scope and the methodology it employs. Urban and regional planning is often referred to as town and country planning, spatial planning, town planning, land use planning, physical planning and city planning. The recurring theme in all these descriptions is that the main task of urban and regional planning is to control the use of limited land. This narrow view of planning and the lack of awareness of the interdependencies of spatial, social and economic developments and the political decisions affecting them has often resulted in a misinterpretation of the role of planners in Jamaica. In fact, there is no real consensus on what planning is all about and there is still the notion that the intention of planning is only physical and can be separated from social and economic aspects of development. It is of interest to note that as planning took root in Britain after the war the main intent was 'to form the future', which implies more than just physical planning (Albers, 1994).

In order to understand the nuances that exist in the definitions mentioned above of planning, it is useful to summarise what constitutes planning. Friedmann (1964) describes planning as being oriented to the future, concerned with the relation of goals to collective decisions, and striving for comprehensiveness of policy and programmes. In general terms, therefore, planning involves a sequence of steps and techniques which result in the formulation of proposals over a specific period of time. While urban and regional planning involves all these elements there is also a geographic dimension. Such planning is also known as spatial planning as it culminates in some form of spatial represen- tation, ranging from a very precise and detailed map to the most general diagram (Hall, 1992). In other words, urban planning or regional planning is a special case of general planning which includes a spatial component.

A brief review of the development of planning theory and practice is relevant in order that the significance of the use of varying terms to describe planning in Jamaica may be understood. It is important to describe how these terms developed and the differences implied in each. It is only through tracing this history of planning that we get a better understanding of the variations that exist. A historical review also places in context Jamaica's position in the evolutionary process and provides some insight into the reasons for the lack of consensus as to what constitutes planning in Jamaica.

URBAN PLANNING

Town planning was the original name prescribed to the discipline when it first emerged in the 1800s. Emphasis was on town planning as efforts were made to improve the housing conditions of the rapidly growing industrial towns. Ebenezer Howard's garden city movement played an important role in shaping British urban planning theory and practice (Ward, 1994). The new towns, Letchworth (1903) and Welwyn (1919) were constructed along the lines set out in Howard's book, *Garden Cities of Tomorrow* (Howard, 1902). By 1905 the various initiatives of land and housing reform and the garden city concept were being integrated into 'a self-conscious town planning movement'. The term itself was conceived in 1905 by John S Nettlefold, the chairman of Birmingham's housing committee (Ward, 1994).

Town and country planning evolved out of Howard's notion that garden cities should link town and country so that the new settlements would have the advantages of both the town (accessibility) and the country (environment), without any of the disadvantages of either (Hardy, 1991). In this regard, Howard proposed that new towns be created outside of the commuter range of the old city, surrounded by a large green belt, accessible to everyone. Both Letchworth and Welwyn were based on this concept. The Town and Country Planning Association evolved from the Garden City and Town Planning Association after the war when there was a demand for planning and public new towns (Hardy, 1991). Town planning was subsumed into town and country planning as there was a growing recognition that a city or urban centre should not be planned in isolation from its hinterland.

The New Towns Act of 1946 was the legislation which facilitated the development of new towns in Britain. The plans for these towns were usually prepared by architect-planner consultants. Land use zoning was fairly strict with housing and industrial areas clearly separated. Physical design standards and open space provision were also clearly detailed (Ward, 1994). The 1947 Town and Country Planning Act was one of the most important pieces of legislation introduced in the urban and regional planning system of Britain. The legislation was important because it allowed for the effective control of land use and new development. It also made possible the delineation of green belts around the larger urban areas in order to contain and regulate their growth.

During the 1960s there was a growing awareness that the 1947 Act was not conducive to meeting the expanding demands required of planning. A number of initiatives were undertaken to address the issue. Foremost among these initiatives was the Planning Advisory Group (PAG) Report of 1965. The report was very instrumental in setting the framework for urban and regional planning and creating linkages between physical and economic planning. The PAG report formed the basis of the 1968 Act, the first major reform of the planning system which was based on the 1947 Act (Ward, 1994). The 1968 Act introduced new concepts for planning which gave greater significance to policy as opposed to the emphasis on physical and land use planning which was integral to the 1947 Act. Another important aspect of the 1968 Town and Country Planning Act was the provision for greater public participation although the exact form this was to take was not clear.

This concept of public participation is a distinguishing feature of the more advisory character of city planning in the United States of America (Foley, 1973). During the 1960s, in the USA there was also a great deal of pressure for more involvement of the people in the process of determining their needs rather than the planner implementing his ideas or carrying out an official policy without the consideration of such needs. This notion of partnership between the people and the state in the planning process has evolved in the United States of America into advocacy planning, where the planner articulates the needs of the voiceless and the disenfranchised (Albers, 1994).

Planning systems and concepts are constantly being adapted to accommodate changing conditions and circumstances. For example, the 1947 Town and Country Planning Act of Britain has been replaced by the Acts of 1968, 1971, 1972 and 1990. These changes in statutory town planning have often been in response to shifts in ideology and policies. In contrast, the planning system in Jamaica has not responded to required changes. New thinking and concepts have been introduced but this has not resulted in any substantial or meaningful change as systems are still firmly entrenched in the 1947 Town and Country Planning Act of Britain. Emphasis is given, therefore, to land use zoning with housing and industrial areas clearly separated, physical design standards, open space provision and development control. It is not surprising therefore that urban and regional planning in Jamaica is referred to as 'land use planning' or 'physical planning' meaning that it is only concerned with the planning of an area's physical structure in an effort to regulate a town's development. Issues such as national urbanisation policies, urban management, public participation etc, are not an integral part of the town planning debate, hence they have not been influential in shaping the policy agenda and remain outside any form of statutory provision.

REGIONAL PLANNING

Although it was some of the earliest urban planners who intro-duced the concept of city regions within the scope of their plans, regional planning as understood today has another meaning. In fact, the Regional Planning Association of America (RPAA) was founded in 1923 by a group of architects and planners who met in New York for regular discussion of urban problems (Friedmann and Weaver, 1979). Metropolitan planning, or metropolitan regionalism as it was sometimes called, was one of the early forerunners of regional planning and involved planning of the entire metropolitan area within the scope of the plan. This concept of metropolitan planning was first advocated by Patrick Geddes who published *Cities in Evolution* in 1915. In this document Geddes stressed the importance of linking the town to its natural region (Hall, 1992). It was the view of the RPAA that the city could only survive with the totality of its regional environment and regional planning was a method that could be used to contain metropolitan growth and re-establish what they called regional balance. The planning strategies of the RPAA was based on decentralisation and the development of new towns was the means through which this would be achieved (Friedmann and Weaver, 1979).

Regional planning theory was influenced not only by metropolitan regionalism and the RPAA, but by the structural shifts in the economy in the 1920s and 1930s. In both Britain and America in the 1920s and 1930s urban-based industrialisation was replacing older industries such as cotton, steel and shipbuilding. This resulted in sharp disparities between regions. For example unemployment was rising in Scotland and Wales in Britain and in the southern states of the United States of America when compared with the rest of the country. A number of initiatives were undertaken to reduce regional imbalances. In Britain the Barlow Commission was appointed in 1937 to investigate the problem and make recommendations on remedial measures. Their terms of reference established an important link between urban and economic problems as the commission was requested to inquire inter alia into the causes which influenced the distribution of the industrial population of Great Britain and to consider what social, economic or strategic disadvantages arise from the concentration of industries or of the industrial population in large towns (Ward, 1994).

Despite these initiatives, the real impetus of regional planning theory did not come until the 1950s and 1960s. This was as a result of a shift in focus from the paradigm of regional resource development to one of economic growth in a spatial dimension (Friedmann and Weaver, 1979). This gave rise to the meaning of regional planning as understood today, i.e. it usually refers to planning which seeks to find solutions to the economic inequalities between regions (Glasson, 1974).

Friedmann and Weaver (1979) point out that the evolution of regional planning since the 1950s has been two-pronged. Along one dimension it refers to economic planning with a view to the development of regions which, for one reason or another, are suffering serious economic problems (Hall, 1992). The second construct is basically concerned with spatial organisation. This dimension of regional planning was particularly attractive to developing countries as its main focus was the spatial integration of the national economy. The basic idea was that urban industrial growth could be diffused to the backward regions of a developing country by concentrating on the infrastructure at selected points – growth centres (or sub-regions) – which had the potential for economic expansion. It was envisaged that through this process primacy would be reduced considerably in developing countries while at the same time growth would occur in secondary towns. The 'spread effects' of development would be generated through-out the country from the principal growth centres of the economy (Rondinelli, 1983).

An unusual contradiction exists in Jamaica between regional theory, regional planning and regional plans. The theoretical underpinning of regional planning is based on the notion that this form of planning is the purview of economic planning. In 1972, when the national economic planning machinery was restructured to establish the National Planning Agency (NPA), a regional planning division was one of five divisions which made up the NPA (Bonnick, 1995). However, regional economic planning never really found its niche as part of the national planning framework and the Regional planning division suffered a series of setbacks which eventually led to its disappearance. The end result is that regional planning as a function has never really taken off although the policy of balanced regional development has remained one of the objectives of successive governments.

On the other hand, however, there has been some recognition of the importance of the need to redress some of the problems of regional disparities. The National Physical Plans 1970–1990 and 1978–1998 recommended the adoption of an urban structure and policy in response to rapid urban growth taking place in the country. This urban policy, the National Settlement Strategy, was to provide the framework through which the capacity of small and intermediate settlements would be strengthened to generate more widespread and equitable development. The fact that the National Settlement Strategy has not been used as a tool to correct the disparities existing in the country stems from the fact that the connection between socio-economic policy and spatial planning is not fully understood. This particular theme will be discussed in greater detail in Chapter VI.

25

Several regional plans have been prepared in Jamaica. Most of these plans are at the scale of the urban region or specially demarcated regions which include the urban centre and its related hinterland. They are essentially concerned with establishing strategies which would guide the spatial direction of future growth and development. They attempt to go beyond the narrow confines of detailed statements referring to future land use proposals by including social policy planning issues such as the housing problem and educational requirements of the population. Despite the fact that the content of these regional plans is broad-based, stressing basic policies rather than land use allocations, there is a notion that these plans are still physical plans fashioned according to typically British tradition.

Planning Practice in Jamaica

Although planners in Jamaica have recognised the changing role of planning over the years and have been involved in promoting issues such as sustainable development, human settlements planning, and local government reform, the planning machinery in the country is still heavily steeped in the earliest paradigm of planning. Inherited from the colonial era, this system of planning still exists today with only minimal changes to scope and method- ology. The system introduced by the Town and Country Planning Act of 1957 was extensively patterned on the 1947 British Act (Nettleford, 1971). As such the planning system created in Jamaica stressed the orderly development of land through land use controls.

Although shifts in this paradigm in the 1970s resulted in the preparation of urban and regional plans, these plans have been used mainly to provide guidelines for applying development control regulations. Very little attention has been given to the importance of spatial planning as a means of guiding growth in a comprehensive manner. In other words, the negative (control) aspects, rather than the positive (growth) aspects, of these plans are those promoted. The plan is not used therefore as a strategic tool to guide growth, but has its focus on zoning and land use controls.

!!! LIMITED SUCCESS !!!

The limited success of the implementation of urban and regional plans as strategic tools for growth and development may also be attributed to two other reasons which revolve around the planning process. First, as funding for development activity is based on plans prepared at a national level by ministries and their agencies, implementation of programmes are directed at the national/sector level, rather than the urban or regional level. Because urban and regional plans are not action oriented, directly linked to investment programmes (capital budgeting), with all costs determined and backed up by serious financing plans they are not suitable for implementation by sector agencies.

The second reason is related to the absence of coordination and integration at the urban and regional levels. At a local level, authorities are primarily concerned with the maintenance of infrastructure and social and community services. On the other hand, projects which affect regional development and are shaping the urban (spatial) network are designed and implemented by sector agencies. Because of the nature of the processes included in the execution of these projects, investment is normally spread throughout the country according to sector priorities set up by different agencies in charge of their implementation. However, these expenditure are not usually spatially coordinated or integrated in time. This approach results in the lack of an area or community focus on which long-term objectives and priorities may be based.

Summary

In conclusion, it may be said that a serious schism exists between planners and the planning machinery. On the one hand, planners have recognised the changing role of planning and several initiatives have been undertaken to meet these demands. (The succeeding chapters of this book will discuss these initiatives and their impact on the planning process in Jamaica.) On the other hand, however, the planning machinery in Jamaica has been slow to change and remains firmly entrenched in a traditional paradigm which places a great deal of emphasis on physical (land use) planning. This latter fact has resulted in urban and regional

NEW

DREAM ?

planning in Jamaica being narrow in scope and concerned only with land use allocations. Planners in Jamaica have been calling for a new interpretation of planning, a theme which is taken up in Chapter VII of this book.

Chapter II

ORIGINS OF PLANNING IN JAMAICA

Urban and regional planning in Jamaica originated from two separate strands, namely, the institution of local government and the housing movement. It is important to note that during the evolutionary process of planning, these two important forces did not coalesce, but rather developed in isolation from each other. This two-tract development of the planning machinery in part accounts for some of the problems being experienced in the planning implementation and development process. As problems arose, new legislation and institutions were introduced to address these issues. While some of these new institutions introduced innovative approaches to deal with the problems, often other difficulties of coordination surfaced. In some instances, legislation gave the new institutions powers which reduced the effectiveness of the already existing organisation. This has not had the overall effect of improving planning practice in Jamaica. These are some of the issues discussed in Chapters II and III. In this chapter we analyse some of the early factors which were responsible for the introduction of planning into the country, while in Chapter III we examine the main pieces of legislation which shaped and influenced urban and regional planning as it exists today.

The Local Government System

THE ORIGIN AND STRUCTURE OF LOCAL GOVERNMENT

The institution of local government has existed in Jamaica for over three hundred years, having been established by the British in 1664. The system which was introduced at that time was copied from the system which then existed in England. It consisted of local authorities which had jurisdiction over their parishes for poor relief, maintenance of roads, support of the clergy (the church had been established), and the maintenance of order (locally). These authorities met in the vestry of the parish church, and hence the system was referred to as the 'vestry system' (Miller, 1996). A comprehensive revision of the system was undertaken between 1867 and 1887, and the existing system was abolished. The new system saw the creation of fourteen local authorities known as parochial boards. These boards comprised both elected members and nominated or ex-officio members chosen by the governor. The elected members were chosen through an electoral system which limited the franchise to the land-owning class and those who were literate. The system that now exists in Jamaica is based largely on the model which was introduced in the period of 1867 to 1887. The only major changes introduced since that time are: the extension of the franchise for electing local representatives in 1947 to include all adults; and the gradual elimination of non-elected members of the councils (Miller, 1996).

The government system in Jamaica is a two-tier system comprising of central government at a national level, and local government authorities at a sub-national or parish level. The local authorities consist of twelve parish councils and the municipal authority of Kingston which is called the Kingston and St Andrew Corporation (KSAC) and incorporates the parishes of Kingston and St Andrew. These thirteen local authorities are part of the system of representative democracy in the country and were created by law. The Parish Councils Law, Chapter 271, and the Kingston and St Andrew Corporation Law, Chapter 192, give legal status to the councils. The KSAC is the only municipal council with city functions clearly defined while the parish councils are ordinary corporations.

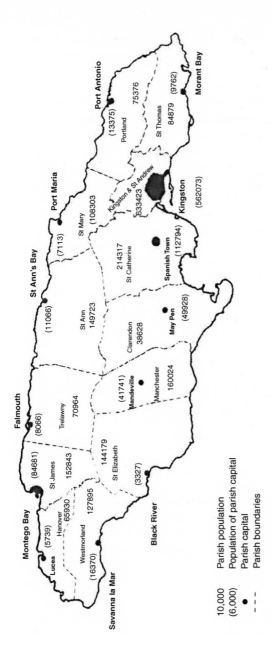

Figure 2.1: The fourteen parishes of Jamaica in 1991 with their populations and parish capitals. All of the parish of Kingston is considered urban and together with the urban sectors of the parish of St Andrew make up the capital city, Kingston or the Kingston Metropolitan Area (KMA).

Montego Bay
Lucea
(5739)
Hanover
65930
Westmorland
127895
Savanna la Mar
(16370)

Falmouth
(8066)
St James
152843
Trelawny
70964

St Elizabeth
144179

Black River
(3327)

St Ann's Bay
(11066)
St Ann
149723

Mandeville
(41741)
Manchester
160024

Clarendon
38628

May Pen
(49928)

Port Maria
(7113)
St Mary
108303

St Catherine
214317

Spanish Town
(112794)

Port Antonio
(13375)
Portland
75376

Kingston & St Andrew
533423

Kingston
(562073)

St Thomas
84879

Morant Bay
(9762)

10,000   Parish population
(6,000)   Population of parish capital
●   Parish capital
– –   Parish boundaries

Councillors are elected directly through secret ballots and the laws which govern these elections are the same as those governing the national electoral procedures. Local government elections are expected to take place every three years, except in extraordinary circumstances when parliament may extend the duration of a council for a specific period. The mayor of the capital of a parish, is elected by his or her colleagues from among the membership of the council at the first meeting in the life of that council; the mayor is also the chairperson of the council. According to the law, the council must meet monthly to discuss and make decisions on the business of the council and reports received from committees. The councils carry out their functions through the committee system and also meet to make regulations and bye-laws which are important for the smooth running of the parish. Local councils are created by specific laws enacted by the national parliament. This means that they cannot act outside of the law and cannot go beyond the power of the law; they would be acting illegally if they did anything not specifically permitted or ordained by the law. This is a very inflexible system and in fact the function of the councils is narrowly prescribed by the law and can be changed at any time by central government.

There are twenty-five laws which define the powers and duties of the councils. Some of the major responsibilities of the councils, such as public health and poor relief, have separate laws. Some of these laws have been revised, but the poor relief law dates back to 1681. Under the public health law the council is also the Local Board of Health. The functions and services for which local authorities have responsibility are either shared with national government ministries and institutions or are basically minor functions such as markets, abattoirs, infirmaries, cemeteries, parks, street lighting and public sanitation. Shared functions include maintenance of the road network, precaution against disasters, planning and the provision of minor water supplies. The councils also perform a number of regulatory functions. In addition to having fairly minor responsibilities, in carrying out its functions local government is often treated as a junior partner in its relationship with central government. For example, it is the council that decides which roads will be fixed in the parish, but only central government may decide that income tax derived from motor vehicle licences will be used for road repair.

THE DECLINE OF LOCAL GOVERNMENT 1970–80

While the national government structure has evolved over the past four decades since independence in 1962, the local government system has not undergone a similar evolution in responding to the needs of the parishes. In fact, the perpetuation of an archaic structure has been responsible in part for the upheavals which have taken place in local government during the past three decades. These upheavals range from the dismantling of a number of functions and responsibilities of the councils during the 1970s and 1980s to attempts to revitalise the local government system in the 1990s.

In the 1960s and at the time of independence, the thirteen local authorities derived approximately 75% of their revenue from local fees and taxes. Even though central government had control of their finances, the thirteen local authorities operated at a profit. At this time the councils were very effective in providing local services and maintaining the local infrastructure for which they had responsibility. In 1974, central government removed the property tax as a source of income from the realm of local government and replaced it with a general assistance grant. With the removal of the property tax local councils no longer had an independent source of revenue which could be used to respond effectively to the growth in expenditure and needs of the parish and the majority of councils had to rely on a long list of minor revenue sources – abattoirs, cemeteries, markets, etc. The councils became increasingly dependent therefore, on central government for their income with weaker councils becoming heavily reliant on government grants. This in turn limited the ability of the local authorities to provide the necessary services.

By not delineating clearly what should constitute the legitimate core revenue bases and by excluding traditional items such as property taxes and motor vehicle licence fees from the parish tax base, central government classified grants to the local authorities for recurrent expenditure into the following categories: General Assistance Grants (comprised of the proceeds from spirit licences, 50% of the revenue from motor vehicle licences, and grants in lieu of rates on government property); Specific Grants (comprised of an amount based on 100% of local expenditure on public health, seventy-five of that spent on poor relief, and 50% of the cost of water supplies maintenance); and Non-Recurrent Grant (an amount to meet the budgetary deficits of the council).

In terms of resource use, expenditure by local authorities is classified as capital or recurrent. Recurrent expenditure covers costs such as administrative staff, overheads, operation and routine maintenance of the various services provided by the councils. Capital expenditure refers to building or installing new infrastructure or superstructure facilities or undertaking comprehensive reconstruction works. During the 1970s central government financed all of the councils' capital expenditure. The dependency on ministries and statutory bodies for funds for capital works led to an under-developed capital budgetary practice of the councils. The capital budget was not in any way linked to the recurrent budget and often a capital budget was not prepared for capital works programmes. In addition, there were no links between the capital budget and development planning. Capital grants were all earmarked for particular programmes such as minor water supplies and beautification projects.

As the dependency of the councils on central government increased, the performance of the councils deteriorated. This led to several studies being commissioned to examine the issue and devise appropriate solutions. At least seven of these studies identified inadequate financing and lack of autonomy as the major factors responsible for the deficiencies of local government. These studies recommended that local authorities should be provided with adequate and independent sources of revenue, and given greater autonomy in managing their own affairs (Miller, 1996). However, very few of the recommendations made in these reports were implemented (Urban Growth and Management Study, 1978). The end result was the continued decline of local government, and in 1985 central government dismantled the local government system, citing poor performance as the major rationale of its action. The former functions and responsibilities of the councils were transferred to central ministries and their agencies. This re-assignment of responsibilities was accompanied by drastic reductions in the staffing and equipment of many councils. Several parish councils were required to transfer most of their road maintenance and workshop machinery and equipment to the central government ministries and agencies. This left the councils with a significantly reduced capacity to address local needs, particularly during the hurricane season.

In addition to re-assigning the responsibilities and functions of local government, 90% of the revenue used to fund local activities was redirected through central government. These changes essentially converted local government into an agency of central government with the responsibility of managing some minor government social programmes, but without adequate resources or incentives for effective implementation.

It was thought that a centralised system would provide improved planning and the utilisation of scarce skilled labour, eliminate duplications, and promote economies of scale and efficiency that would benefit the country as a whole. In reality, however, the results were quite different. During this same period the country was undergoing a series of structural adjustment programmes. The effects of the international recession were exacerbated by the collapse of the bauxite and aluminium market – the country's main export. Because of the resource constraints and organisational problems, the expanded role of central government agencies did not develop as envisaged. Central government was unable to deliver and not only did the local government system experience a serious decline, but the combined functions, with the exception of solid waste management, suffered as a result (Miller, 1996).

The success of solid waste management during the period was due, in large measure, to the significant increase in resources assigned to the function and in part to the organisational structure set up to manage garbage collection and disposal. Prior to 1985, refuse collection and disposal and street sweeping services were operated by the public cleansing department of the councils. In 1986, these services were transferred to the ministry of local government and works and operational responsibility was assigned to five public sector companies whose responsibilities also included parks and markets.

However, apart from the parks and markets' companies, the functions transferred to central agencies experienced serious deterioration. The loss of direct revenue and major service responsibility left the councils with a diminished leadership role in which they only acted as conduits for funding requests and transfers, while they carried out welfare functions. They no longer had the resources to manage the parochial road network and minor water supplies, or to maintain and expand other services.

Local Reform of the 1990s

In 1989 a new government was elected to power on a mandate which included a commitment to the restoration of a strong local government system and to the implementation of the Local Government Reform Programme (Miller, 1996). The principal objectives of this programme as outlined in 1993 are to broaden the democratic process, empower local citizens to play a greater role in the management of their own development and improve the quality, cost-effectiveness and responsiveness of local services, regulatory functions and elected officials (Ministry Paper 8/93, 1993).

In order to achieve these overall development objectives the LGRP seeks inter alia to: restore to the parish councils and the Kingston and St Andrew Corporation (KSAC) the functions and responsibilities which have been eroded since the early 1980s; establish new financing arrangements which will allow the flow of adequate and independent sources of revenue to the councils and grant them control over such revenue; upgrade the institutional capability of the local authorities; carry out a comprehensive revision of outdated legislation; and identify a better distribution of delivery of services between central government, local government, NGOs, CBOs and the private sector (Ministry Paper 8/93, 1993).

Several initiatives have been undertaken as part of the LGRP. Most of the functions which were taken away from the councils have now been returned and financial and legal reforms have been instituted to ensure local government revenue autonomy. In this regard, the granting of greater autonomy to parish councils and the KSAC in the setting and adjustment of licence fees and user charges in respect of the services and regulatory functions for which councils are responsible, has resulted in an increase in the share of revenue collected from these sources. The upgrading of the level of technical and managerial staff of the councils is being undertaken through improved salaries and training.

One of the major outcomes of the LGRP has been the establishment of the parochial revenue fund, which constitutes the major component of the new arrangements for the financing of local government. All revenues from property taxes, spirit licences and trade licences and two thirds of the revenue from motor vehicle licences are lodged into the Parochial Revenue Fund instead of going into the formerly centralised consolidate fund, thus providing the councils with designated sources of income. Ninety per cent of the property taxes collected in the parishes goes back to the parish of origin. However, 10% is retained in an equalisation fund to go to the smaller parishes whose property taxes are marginal. With regard to motor vehicle licence fees, 25% is returned to the parish of origin and the other 75% placed in a pool and distributed according to the total mileage of parochial roads in each parish.

As a consequence of the implementation of the above-mentioned reform measures, parish councils and the KSAC generated 54% of its budgeted expenditure from these sources in the financial year of 1998/99. This compares to councils generating only 5% prior to reform while 95% came in the form of central government grants (McHardy, 1999). The point must be made, however, that even with the establishment of the parochial revenue fund the most significant share of council revenue (property taxes, motor vehicle, spirit, and trade licences) is money collected by the inland revenue department of central government and transferred to the KSAC and parish councils. This still leaves the councils dependent on central government for the collection of its revenue. New arrangements with the inland revenue department to improve revenue collections from spirit and trade licences and to transfer responsibility for the overall management of these sources to the parish councils and the KSAC were implemented in 1999 with amendments to the Spirit Licences Act. This is expected to significantly increase revenue flows from these sources and give the councils a central role in overseeing this exercise.

A major challenge facing the LGRP is that of enhancing the revenue of the local authorities. According to data from the inland revenue department, over US $7.7 million is outstanding and due to the councils from property taxes (Reid, 1996). The revenue from property taxes is designated to cover street lighting, public sanitation and parks and beautification. What is clear, however, is that this source will not be adequate to cover the related expenses. Furthermore, even if all the money due on the property tax was collected, councils would still be faced with a deficit.

Another major outcome of the LGRP is the Parish Infrastructure Development Programme (PIDP). With assistance from the Inter-American Development Bank (IDB), the Japanese Government, the United Nations Development Programme (UNDP) and the World Bank, the PIDP has been designed as the main vehicle for achieving the objectives of the LGRP. The PIDP will be financed with a loan of US $35 million from the IDB and counterpart funds from the Government of Jamaica amounting to US $15 million. The IDB loan will finance two components: institutional strengthening and technical assistance; and investment in parish infrastructure. Investment in the first component will support necessary legal and institutional reforms under the LGRP. The second component would finance the rehabilitation of basic infrastructure for which the councils have responsibility. This includes the rehabilitation of the parochial road and drainage systems, minor water supplies, solid waste management and the upgrading of facilities such as markets and abattoirs (IDB Projects vol. VI no. 8, 1999).

While the LGRP will undoubtedly strengthen the administrative and technical capacity of the local authorities to manage and maintain infrastructure and improve the delivery of social services it may be argued that the reform process has not gone far enough. The reform process has been laid on a system of government dating back to 1867. Absent from the LGRP are issues such as governance and urban management; decentralisation; rationalisation of relationships between local government and other levels of public administration; and the development of new sources of financing. Questions must be raised about the effectiveness of a system which does not recognise the importance of governance of the larger towns in the country. The system set up in 1867 was at a time when the country was essentially rural. Since then the small rural centres have evolved into large townships and urban centres. According to the 1990 census of Jamaica, approximately half (52.3%) of the population live in urban areas. It must be assumed that at some stage of this evolutionary process from rural to urban, Jamaica's towns and cities would have grown rapidly, exhausting the capability of the extant local government system to respond to their constituencies. The reduction of primacy in Jamaica provides clear evidence of the rapid growth of its urban centres. The primary index declined from 7.2 in 1960 to 2.2 in 1990 (Portes et al, 1997). A major part of the crisis in local government arose from the systemic crisis in the ability of the institution of local governments to evolve in a manner consistent with the requirements of emerging problems and opportunities. We will return to this theme when we examine planned decentralisation in Chapter IV.

Planning Functions of the Local Authorities

Several pieces of legislation govern the management, planning and use of land in Jamaica. These laws confer wide areas of jurisdiction on the agencies on whom the particular responsibilities rest. However, conflicting and overlapping responsibilities among various government agencies and statutory bodies often cause confusion, lack of coordination, unclear responsibilities and neglect of duties. The planning functions and responsibilities of the local authorities are governed by laws which, like the local government system, were introduced many years ago. None of these laws have undergone any significant reform to reflect the local culture, resource system and economy more clearly, and as a result they are now inappropriate and difficult to enforce.

The local authorities have responsibility for the subdivision of land and the granting of permission for the erection of buildings.

Improvement aimed at enhancing the efficiency and quality of service in the processing of building and subdivision applications is one of the stated objectives of the Local Government Reform Programme. The land development process has not changed significantly for the last forty years while social, economic and political forces have undergone substantial change. The process has become extremely cumbersome and thwart with excessive delays. Subdivision regulations are rigid and in many respects unclear. New building regulations need to be enforced, making the use of the National Building Code mandatory.

Changes in the regulatory framework will have to be made if the performance of the local authorities is to improve and if they are to increase their ability to meet residents' needs. These changes include: reducing the complexity and time requirements of land use and development controls; improving institutional coordination; improving institutional capability at a local level; and decentralisation of the approval process.

SUBDIVISION OF LAND

The subdivision of land in Jamaica is governed by the Local Improvements Act which was enacted in 1914 (Chapter 227 as amended). Section 4, paragraphs 4 and 5 of this Act defines subdivision as follows:

> For the purpose of this Act a person shall be deemed to lay out or sub-divide land for the purposes of building thereon or for sale, if he sells or offers for sale any part of such land whereon a house or other building may be erected, or if he shall form the foundations of a house or other building thereon, in such a manner and in such a position so that such house or other building will or may become one of two or more houses or other buildings erected on such land.
>
> Sale with its grammatical variations and cognate expressions includes exchange, gift or other disposition affecting the fee simple and lease for any term (including renewals thereunder) or any letting or any licence whereby the land may be used for building purposes, and also includes any disposition affecting the leasehold interest under any such lease as aforesaid.

Milton Brown → councillor for May Pen.

The Act also stipulates that every person who intends to subdivide land must submit to the parish council or the KSAC a map showing the proposed layout. Such a map must show proposed streets and the division into lots and be accompanied by specifications of how streets are to be constructed, the nature of sewers, water pipes, gas pipes and lighting mains. It should be drawn to scale and set forth all particulars which the local planning authorities may, by regulation, prescribe.

Procedures for Subdivision Applications

The procedure for applying for permission to subdivide land is set out in Figure 2.2. Applications (layout plans, location diagrams and application forms) for the subdivision of land are submitted to the secretary of the parish council or the town clerk of the KSAC. The councils, in turn, must submit these documents to the Chief Technical Director of the Ministry Of Transport And Works and the Government Town Planner (Town Planning Department). The advice of these two agencies cannot be rejected by a local planning authority without allowing them a hearing (Section 10, Local Improvements Act). Once the preliminary checks of the application have been completed, one copy is submitted to the Superintendent of Roads and Works (Ministry of Transport and Works) in the parish and the remaining copies forwarded to the Government Town Planner (GTP).

After the application has been received by the Town Planning Department (TPD), it is recorded and plotted in the department's map registry and sent to the development control section for assessment. Depending on location, size and type of development, the TPD will send the application to other agencies for review although there are no legal requirements to do so. The Town Planning Department makes its own field inspection and analysis and also coordinates the response to the other agencies before a recommendation on the proposal is made by the GTP.

Where the application comprises a subdivision in excess of ten lots, it has also become the practice for the application to be referred to a subdivisions committee. This committee is made up of representatives from many of the same referral agencies involved in the first review, making the process somewhat

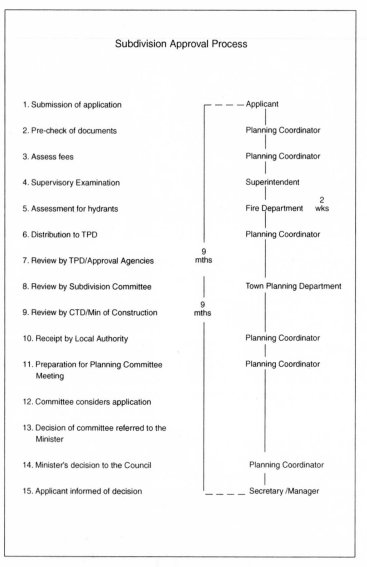

Figure 2.2: Charting the subdivision review process. The process has been the subject of much criticism as being too slow. Measures are being instituted in the hope that the process would be completed within sixty days.

redundant. These advisory agencies investigate and comment on the application, after which the proposal is put on the agenda for a meeting of the committee. A decision on the application may be deferred if any agency needs to carry out further studies or investigations, or if more information is required of the applicant. The recommendation of the committee is then transmitted to the local authority (KSAC or parish council) for a decision. For subdivisions containing ten lots or less, the GTP will respond to the local authority without any reference to the subdivision committee. The comments of the Chief Technical Director (Ministry of Transport and Works) is sought in all instances, in order to comply with the statutory requirements.

The decision of a local planning authority must be sanctioned by the minister responsible for the administration of the Local Improvements Act whose decision is final. This decision is conveyed to the applicant by the local authority. If any application for subdivision is refused by the KSAC or parish council, an applicant may appeal to the minister within twenty-one days of the decision. Appeals should comply with the Local Improvements (Appeals) Rules of 1959.

Improving the Subdivision Approval Process

The subdivision approval process as required by law is cumbersome but has been made even more complicated by external reviews (Kingsley et al, 1989). Between 1981 and 1986, the average subdivision application took 171 days to process, 42 days inside the TPD and 129 days with the outside referral agencies (Kingsley et al, 1989). Thus, the most serious problem was with the referral agencies. Added to this delay, are those which take place at local authority level making the administrative process of receiving, examining and deciding on applications thwart with procedural delays. This tedious process of approval for subdivisions adds substantially to the cost of development which in turn results in illegal development. Estimates indicate that approximately 75% of development takes place outside of the approval process.

Kingsley et al, (1989) attribute the subdivision referral problem to the following:

43

1. None of the referral agencies have written standards to guide their decisions about applications and thus there are no guidelines for developers regarding the criteria on which their applications would be evaluated.

2. Most of the agencies make independent visits to see the sites, which is more costly than joint visits and reduces the benefits of integrated deliberation of the proposed plan.

3. There is a considerable amount of work duplication in some areas. For example, three different agencies review the sanitation aspects of an application.

4. The process requires a considerable amount of unnecessary paperwork as each referral agency has to establish its own system of tracking files that have been sent to them. This often leads to files being misplaced or lost and substantial delays in the search for files.

5. Delays are often caused by resource problems (lack of staff and equipment).

6. Many agencies expend more time and expertise than the exercise requires. For example, in several agencies matters which could be handled by junior staff are being dealt with by senior professionals.

The introduction of computerised applications tracking and management systems at the KSAC and parish councils will provide an opportunity for the proper management of the approval process at the local level. Currently, all councils maintain a system of tracking the subdivision approval process, however, this process varies between councils. Under the Local Government Reform Programme a computerised system is being introduced to all councils. This system will enable the following: the standardisation of procedures for the processing of applications across all the councils; a reduction in bureaucracy in the system by maintaining one register, rather than having several registers recording different parts of the process (e.g. one register to record the application, another to give details on the application, a third to record approval); the maintaining of a register which allows for tracking the application as it moves through the system; the maintaining of a register which allows for the operation of monthly reports on the status of an application (this information can only be obtained from individual files and thus the status is only known after research upon enquiries from the applicant); and the formalisation of procedures for establishing time limits and reports to guide the internal movement of the application in the council (McHardy, 1997c).

Efforts are now being made to reform the system of approval, approximately ten years after Kingsley et al (1989) made their recommendations. Improvements to the subdivisions approval process began in August 1998 and are aimed primarily at reducing the time taken to process applications for subdivision to no more than ninety days. These improvements include: TPD developing a new checklist to guide local authorities through the pre-consultation process with applicants; utilising professionals (engineers, architects) to perform site inspections and thus reduce delays caused by staff shortages at TPD and the local authorities; and improvements in the administrative procedures of the referral agencies. In addition, the local government has implemented a quarterly monitoring report system to review outstanding cases at the TPD and the referral agencies. Steps are also being taken to reduce the time taken for the approval of applications by the Natural Resources Conservation Authority (NRCA) in line with the projected ninety-day period being pursued by other planning agencies.

Kingsley et al (1989), also make recommendations for changes in the Local Improvements Act in line with the objective of expediting the subdivision review process. The first would be to remove the explicit legal requirement that the Chief Technical Director (Ministry of Transport and Works) must review all applications. With regard to the second, the requirement concerning the minister's review of applications after the council has taken its decision, Kingsley et al, 1989, wrote:

> This latter provision is one of the more wasteful elements in the present system. The parishes are forced to go through the paper work entailed in transmitting the applications to the Minister, they are logged in and tracked by his office, and he must then personally sign every one though in most cases the parish

decision conforms to the advice previously given by his own staff (the TPD).

No action has been taken on these recommendations although the proposed amendments would not have eliminated the minister's right to review any and all applications if he so desires, but it would have given him the discretion to eliminate reviews where the council's decision does not conflict with TPD advice. In other words, the parishes would be notified that they could act directly in such cases without his authorisation. The entire legal basis for planning is being reformed and this will be dealt with in Chapter III. However, while the reform process is being modified the length of time required for approval of subdivisions would have been reduced further with the amendment of this statutory requirement.

However, despite the implementation of measures to improve the approval process it is still seen as being too slow. The ninety-day period is seen as a major deterrent to investment in the country, as revenue is being lost while development projects are in limbo for years awaiting approval. In this regard, therefore, the NRCA, TPD and the Land Development and Utilisation Commission (LDUC) are to be merged into a National Environmental Planning Agency. Additionally, the Survey Department and the Titles Office are to be merged to reduce the length of time required to obtain a registered title. The government hopes that with the mergers, the process will be further reduced from ninety days to sixty days.

Decentralisation of the Subdivision Approval Process

An issue which has not been given enough consideration is that of the decentralisation of the approval process. It is significant to note that under the Local Improvements Act, the subdivision approval process is the responsibility of the local authorities. The law clearly states that all persons requiring to subdivide land must ensure that all specifications, plans, sections and estimates must comprise the particulars required by regulations made by the council. Although the local authorities have the power to set regulations for the process, they have never really done so. The intent of the Local Improvements Act was for a locally managed service, not control of the process by central government as it now stands. The main rationale given for increasing central control is the lack of expertise at a local level. During the 1980s, when some of the planning powers of the local authorities were transferred to central government, lack of clarity regarding jurisdictional responsibility coupled with a severely reduced staff complement and crippling resource problems often led to a neglect of duties on the part of the councils. This added fuel to the notion that more control at a central level would be the best way to deal with the issue of councils lacking the requisite skills. However, the core of the local government reform process envisages a greater role for local authorities in the development and management of their respective areas.

The point has been made that the major factor contributing to the lengthy approval process is the requirement that all subdivision applications must be referred to the GTP. It is at this stage of the process that the applications get held up as a result of the complex referral system adopted by the TPD. The proposed merger of the TPD, NRCA and LDUC is supposed to improve the system by introducing a 'one-stop facility'. This process will not result, however, in increased participation on the part of the local authorities. Decentralisation of the subdivision approval process would reduce redundant reviews in the system and expedite application processing. One approach to reform therefore, would be to ensure that all applications under ten lots be dealt with at a local level in order to reduce the circuitous route taken by them. The route is circuitous for many reasons. The application is submitted to the referral agency by the TPD, the head office of this agency in turn submits the application to its parish office for assessment. This assessment is returned to the head office in Kingston for a recommendation to be submitted to the TPD. In a decentralised approach, the TPD would then be able to shift its focus from concentration on development control and subdivision approval to developing and monitoring more long-term strategies that satisfy the broader goals of regional development which are comprehensive and can provide guidelines for investment at both central and local levels. A shift in focus would be possible as approximately 65–70% of subdivision applications are for ten lots and under (McHardy, 1994). General guidelines provided by the TPD would assist the local authorities in identifying 'non-sensitive zones' where subdivisions of ten lots may take place without referring applications to the TPD. This would enhance the decentralisation process as the councils could work with the local offices of the referral agencies in getting advice on subdivisions. This would result in a shorter time span in the approval of subdivisions as much of the bureaucracy in the system would be eliminated.

BUILDING REGULATIONS

The Parish Councils Building Act gives power to the parish council to make bye-laws for the erection, alteration and repair of buildings within the limits of any town or any rural area defined by the parish council. The building bye-laws of the parish councils and the Building Act of the KSAC are used to guide building activity in Jamaica. The building bye-laws of the parishes were enacted in 1949 while the KSAC Building Act was enacted in 1908 and revised periodically. The laws and regulations (made under the laws) prescribe detailed construction procedures for buildings in accordance with the technologies at the time.

The engineers and architects using the regulations found conflicts between the regulations, current building practices and use of available materials. The Government of Jamaica, recognising the need for a comprehensive building code, established a working committee in 1981, to draft such a code taking into account current advances in building technologies and the need to ensure that buildings are properly designed to withstand hurricane and earthquake hazards (Wason, 1984). In 1982, the Cabinet gave its approval for the building code to be published as a policy document, pending the enactment of legislation to provide for the building code.

The code, as currently published, does not contain a section on administration of the code or the administration and enforcement of the existing building laws in each parish still applies. The building code although not incorporated into law is being used by architects and engineers, and their experiences in the use of the code is reported to the Bureau of Standards which regularly

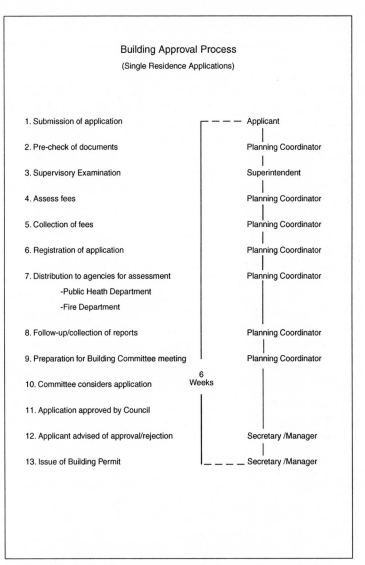

Figure 2.3: The building approval process for single residence applications.
For more complex developments the local authorities usually refer
these to the Town Planning Department.

updates the document through a standing committee. It is intended that the code will be applied to all buildings, and the sections on administration and enforcement will be customised for use in the parishes.

Because most provisions in the building regulations relate to technology available in 1949 when the regulations were produced, there is a tendency to ignore the outdated provisions, thus, building structures are inspected only for general compliance with accepted engineering principles and the parochial building law. In addition, most councils also rely on the competence of the architects and engineers who designed the buildings and therefore do not carry out detailed checks.

Housing Policies and Spatial Planning

Spatial planning in Jamaica was not only introduced through the local government system but also has its roots in the response to the problems associated with urbanisation, particularly in the capital city. The Town and Country Planning Act was promulgated at a time when there was a growing concern about the social and economic conditions prevailing in the country and national planning was emerging as the framework for economic development. The basic framework for national planning was established in the 1940s as the vehicle for the implementation of the recommendations of the Moyne Commission (Mills, 1995). This commission was set up to investigate the underlying causes which led to civil disturbances which occurred in the British West Indies between 1935 and 1938. The recommendations of the commission led to the preparation in 1945 of the ten-year development plan (1945–56). The plan was prepared by the Colonial Secretariat to guide the development expenditures being made by the British Government as a result of the recommendations of the Commission. This plan set the framework for the development of national planning in the country and the modern paradigm of economic planning (Mills, 1995).

Although town and country planning was introduced at a time when economic planning was in its formative years, these two streams of planning – economic and spatial – evolved separately.

Despite many efforts to bring about an understanding between the spatial ramifications of economic decisions, these two branches still remain far apart and disjointed. Settlement development is often considered a spin-off of economic development and the inextricable interdependence between where people live and where development takes place is not recognised. Additionally, the introduction of planning legislation though a route other than the local government system has resulted in the lack of harmonisation of the various pieces of legislation and the processes they govern. Adequate provision of housing for low-income households has been one of the basic goals of housing policy in Jamaica. However, rapid population growth and urbanisation have made the provision of shelter one of the most difficult tasks faced by successive governments.

GROWTH OF THE KINGSTON METROPOLITAN AREA

Period Prior to 1943

Kingston has the distinction of being one of the oldest cities established by the British in the New World. Christian Lilly has been credited with the design of the town plan for Kingston although the minutes of the Council of Jamaica indicate that John Goffe devised the scheme (Clarke, 1975). The plan of Kingston was geometrical and took the shape of a parallelogram. Measuring three quarters of a mile in length from north to south and half a mile in breadth, it covered 240 acres (97.1 hectares) (Clarke, 1975). Straight streets cut across one another at right angles and divided the parallelogram into a grid or chessboard pattern. The rectangular street blocks were 97.5 metres wide and were bisected by lanes which ran from north to south. The depth of each building lot was 45.7 metres and the frontage 15.2 metres (Clarke, 1975).

The growth of the Kingston Metropolitan Area has taken the form of adding subdivisions to the city to meet the demand for houses according to the increase in the city's population. The most marked expansion, bringing the city's population up to the present level, began in the 1920s and was mainly brought on by the advent of motor transport which increased centralisation of the island's communication. Also important was the inability of agriculture to absorb the growing population which was increasing at about 1.5% per year (Urban Growth and Management Study, 1978).

By 1911, the areas which were available for peasant cultivation were becoming increasingly scarce and in addition improved industrial techniques had reduced the demand for rural labour. These factors, plus rapid population growth brought about by improved public health and reduced opportunities for emigration, resulted in high man-to-land ratios in the rural areas and fuelled the movement of people away from the rural areas to Kingston. This increase was accelerated by an inflow of returned emigrants in the years of depression. Official records of migration show a net immigration of 28,000 between 1928 and 1943, many of whom settled in Kingston. The rapid growth of Kingston continued in the period of 1921 to 1943, approximately at a rate of 4.3% per annum (Urban Growth and Management Study, 1978).

The population of Kingston more than doubled between 1921 and 1943. This growth was accommodated both by the concentration of even larger numbers within the older parts of the city and by suburban expansion on the Liguanea Plain (Clarke, 1975). The most important movement of population within the city was the outflow of migrants from the parish of Kingston to the suburbs of St Andrew. The cross-town movement probably involved two groups of migrants and two different reception areas. The first group comprised persons living in Kingston in the better, low-density residential suburbs that extended northward. The second settled in the improvised yards adjacent to the Spanish Town Road in West Kingston (Clarke, 1975). Conditions in these yards and tenements were cramped and decrepit as reported by the Moyne Commission in 1938:

> It is no exaggeration to say that the poorest parts of most towns and in many of the country districts a majority of the houses is largely made of rusty corrugated iron and unsound boarding; quite often the original floor has disappeared and only the earth remains, its surface so trampled that it is impervious to any rain which may penetrate through a leaking roof; sanitation in any form and water supply are unknown in such premises, and in many cases no light can enter when the door is closed. These

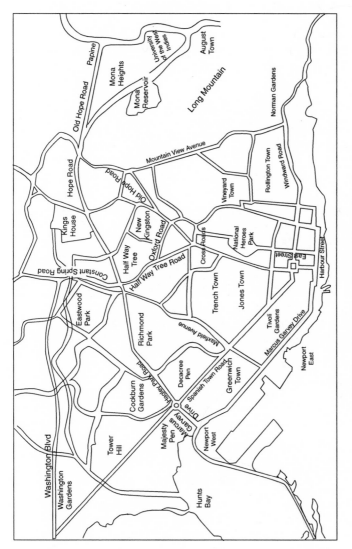

Figure 2.4: Map showing Kingston Metropolitan Area.

decrepit homes, more often than not, are seriously overcrowded, and it is not surprising that some of them are dirty and verminous in spite of the praiseworthy efforts of the inhabitants to keep them clean.

In order to deal with the deteriorating housing situation, the Central Housing Authority (CHA) was formed in 1937, replacing the Central Housing Advisory Board. This was the first national-level housing body to be formed and it focused its attention on slum clearance and re-housing. In 1939, the Slum Clearance and Housing Law was passed. The CHA's first operations were in Kingston and concentrated on slum clearance schemes which included rented housing in the form of multifamily units or tenement blocks of one- or two-storey buildings containing one- and two-room apartments, sharing communal cooking and washing facilities and detached cottages for sale.

1943 to 1960

The trends set in the preceding period intensified during the intercensal period of 1943 to 1960. The population of Kingston and St Andrew almost doubled between 1943 and 1960, although this growth was concentrated in St Andrew (133%), while Kingston experienced a growth of only 12%. The overall growth of Kingston and St Andrew for this period was 85% (Urban Growth and Management Study, 1987). Internal migration played a major role in the growth of the city's population with approxi-mately 43–45% of the population coming from parishes other than Kingston and St Andrew. The net gain of Kingston and St Andrew represented a movement in the intercensal period of 85,000 persons, or about 5,000 per year (Urban Growth and Management Study).

The rapid physical expansion of the city in this period was linked closely to population growth and set in motion the following trends. First, there was a northerly and north-easterly upper-class suburban movement over the St Andrew Plains towards Stony Hill. Since there was no movement into the western part of the Liguanea Plains, development of public transportation assumed migration would be in the eastern half of

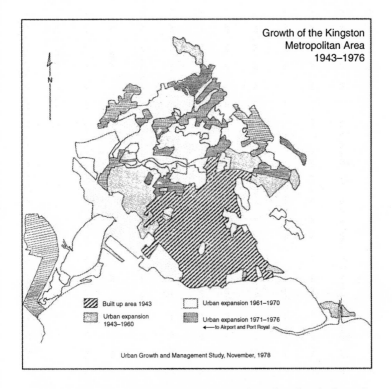

Figure 2.5: The growth of Kingston between 1943 and 1976 has taken the form of adding subdivisions to the city. Since then, however, most development has taken the form of 'infill', i.e. construction of apartments and townhouses at higher densities on the former larger lots.

the city and the transportation routes reinforced the tendency to regard the east as desirable.

Secondly, there was an easterly and northern movement of middle-class suburbanisation following in the wake of the upper-class movement. Thirdly, the rapid growth of population in the preceding period led to serious overcrowding in the urban areas, with no corresponding expansion of social overhead capital. Hence in western Kingston and St Andrew, a slum area developed and there was a vague expansion northwards. Fourthly, there began a rudimentary industrial development in the west of Kingston (Urban Growth and Management Study, 1978).

During this period, middle-income housing resulted mainly from private construction undertaken by individuals as vacant or rural lands were subdivided, mainly in the north and north-eastern sector of the city. Most of the areas opened up in this way were low density, for middle- and upper-income populations. Appearing in this period was a new type of housing, commonly described as informal or squatter settlements. In 1958, when the government began work on the Sandy Gully drainage scheme, extensive areas of poor housing developed along the gully in the western sector. Another large area of poor housing was found south of the Constant Spring Gully and the Barbican Gully in the northern sector of the city.

Post 1960s

In the 1970s further structural changes took place in the city which are still continuing today. First, one of the major changes taking place is in the areas adjoining the CBD. This change involves the invasion (often illegal) of commercial and industrial activity into formerly residential areas, resulting in mixed land uses. The other major structural change has been the infilling of the city. Kingston is hemmed in on the north by the Blue Mountains and in the south by Kingston Harbour and as a result large tracts of land have become increasingly unavailable for urban expansion. Consequently, urban development has spread into the adjoining parishes, particularly the parish of St Catherine while infilling is taking place in the city. Within the low density northern sector of the city, which was once the home of the wealthy, the larger lots have been subdivided into towns and apartments, thus increasing the density of these areas. Most of these areas are now occupied by middle- and upper-middle income groups as the wealthy flee to the hills surrounding the city.

Housing Policies and Town Planning 1947–54

Both private and government housing construction were at a high level in Kingston and suburban St Andrew. The increasingly active role played by government in slum clearance and housing in Kingston, and the rapid expansion of the city, led to an understanding of the need to promote orderly change in the city. In 1947, a town planning adviser, an architect, was appointed and a town planning branch of the CHA was established in 1948. In 1947, the town planning adviser prepared a land use map of Kingston. This map had only two land use categories, residential and non-residential and indicated the limits of the built-up area of Kingston and the expansion of suburbs into St Andrew (Clarke, 1995). Despite the preparation of this map, the town planning adviser's functions related mainly to housing. In 1949 the town planning adviser was appointed as a member of the CHA and became the government's chief adviser in the formulation and implementation of housing policy. He was the first qualified architect to design a housing scheme, as schemes until this time were designed by builders. The scheme was a two-storey tenement structure, known as 'White Wing City' (Tower Hill) which was constructed in 1948 on the Spanish Town Road in western Kingston.

In 1951, the British government provided £250,000 to assist Jamaicans repair and rebuild houses after a severe hurricane destroyed or damaged 75,000 homes. The devastation wreaked on the housing stock was blamed on poor planning and lack of maintenance. Four organisations were involved in the reconstruction programme. The Hurricane Housing Organisation (HHO) designed and produced the prefabricated units; the Hurricane Housing Committee coordinated activities; the Tribunal issued application forms, investigated applications and selected beneficiaries; and the Agricultural Loan Societies Board administered the mortgages.

The first relief scheme established was the Emergency

Building Supplies scheme which assisted people who were unable to help themselves. In the first phase 47,000 families benefited. The other three schemes were permanent loan schemes. The building programme under the Rural and Urban Schemes was carried out by the HHO, while in the case of the Lower and Middle Income Groups Scheme, the HHO distributed materials and supervised repairs. All schemes except the Urban Scheme were self-help schemes. The Social Welfare Commission and the Council of Voluntary Social Services were requested to inform people as to how the schemes worked and the criteria to benefit under each.

During the next eight years, the HHO built a total of 7,500 houses of which 2,700 were located in the KMA. This compares with approximately 1,171 units constructed as part of the government housing schemes (260 tenements for rent and 911 cottages for sale) during the period of 1946 to 1951 (Clarke, 1975). In other areas in the KMA, houses were constructed according to specifications set out under the urban scheme. At Trench Town large dwellings were provided for multiple accommodation (tenements and terraced housing). Apartments were located on the Spanish Town Road near Cockburn Pen, but most of the facilities in this scheme were provided on a shared basis, as they also were at Majesty Pen. Majesty Pen was one of the worst designed of the schemes. Households were supplied with barrack-like blocks of two-storey, one-room units, with communal kitchen and bathroom facilities.

In 1952, the Executive Council sought to examine ways in which the cost of housing to middle-class families could be reduced as there were limited funds available for mortgage financing either through the seventeen registered building societies or from one's own funds. A committee was appointed under the chairmanship of the town planner and members included the manager of the CHA, the Chief Engineer of the city of Kingston, two architects from the Public Works Department, four private architects and four private builders. The committee submitted its report in June 1954 and recommended three housing designs for middle-income earners. With the Government Town Planner chairing this committee the functions of the town planner were still inextricably linked to housing.

It was not until 1954 that a Town Planning Department was established. This department was given no more than consultative powers, and the collection and mapping of information, with the exception of that relating to land use and population, was never undertaken (Clarke, 1975). In 1954, the Town Planning Department revised the land use map of Kingston but there was no strategy in place to link housing policies to land use in the city. The main focus of the department continued to be adviser in slum clearance and housing. No attempt was made to integrate slum clearance schemes and housing in general into wider projects of comprehensive development. Thus the lines of division between housing and town planning were being demarcated at this time, despite the fact that the Government Town Planner was connected with policy positions related to both land use and housing.

Development of the Planning Machinery

NATIONAL ECONOMIC PLANNING

This change of government in 1955 had a major impact on the development of the planning machinery in Jamaica. The Central Planning Unit (CPU) was established in 1955. In addition to providing advice to the Chief Minister, its main task was the preparation of the second ten year plan, the National Plan for Jamaica (1957–67).

The five-year Independence Plan (1963–68), was formulated by the CPU in 1963 to supersede the previous ten-year plan. Another five-year plan covering the period of 1970 to 1975 was completed but never implemented as a new government was elected to power in 1972. In that same year the CPU was reorganised to form the National Planning Agency. The NPA did not assume, however, the overall responsibility for national development planning. This was mainly as a result of NPA not coordinating the capital budget or linking the budget to a medium-term development plan (Bonnick, 1995). This was due in part to the emphasis placed on sector strategies rather than overall national planning. Thus there was an agriculture sector strategy with the responsibility for its preparation residing with the agriculture planning unit of the Ministry of Agriculture (Bonnick, 1995). Part of the reason was also the current international economic environment which required NPA to carry-out day-to-day macroeconomic management rather than long-term plans (Bonnick, 1995).

It was not until 1980 that the NPA returned to long-term planning with the preparation of a five-year development plan for the period 1978–82. Despite this, however, this plan was not implemented, once again because of a change of government in 1980. The new government focused on economic stabilisation and structural adjustment which was linked to a three-year rollover plan. The government also embarked on restructuring of the NPA to form the Planning Institute of Jamaica (PIOJ), broadening its role to take on the new responsibilities.

In 1989 a new government was elected to power and in 1990 the PIOJ prepared another five-year development plan for the period of 1990–95. However, the prevailing economic circumstances of the country have made the implementation of long-term plans difficult. In addition, the system of sector planning has become so firmly entrenched that most sector ministries prepare their own plans and the PIOJ coordinates these sector development plans with a view to facilitate the consistent implementation of projects and programmes.

HOUSING AND TOWN AND COUNTRY PLANNING

Amendments to the Housing Act

Adequate provision of housing for low-income households was one of the basic goals of policy of the government elected in 1955. Legislation to combat slums and policies to deal with the housing problem were introduced long before the advent of national planning. Therefore, in an effort to deal with the provision of shelter brought about by rapid population growth and urbanisation, the newly elected government utilised the system already in place. It repealed the Slum Clearance and Housing Act of 1939 and replaced it with the Housing Act of 1955. This Act allowed for the appointment of a Director of Housing and in 1956 the HHO and CHA were merged to form the department of housing in the Ministry of Housing and Social Welfare. With the establishment of the Department of Housing, a Chief Architect was appointed to oversee a staff of mainly building technicians, as policy formulation resided with the Ministry of Housing and Social Welfare and the office of the Town Planner. Prior to the establishment of the Department of Housing, in 1954, the town planning adviser post was upgraded to Government Town Planner and his office expanded to include the posts of Deputy Government Town Planner and Architect. The Deputy Government Town Planner was an architect from Britain as was the Town Planner, however, both the Chief Architect in the Department of Housing and the Architect in the office of the Government Town Planner were Jamaicans.

Housing Policies and Town Planning Prior to 1957

In order to deal with the housing problems of Kingston, the Ministry of Housing and Social Welfare and the office of the Government Town Planner formulated policies which were directed at ridding the city of the low density squatter areas and at the same time would permit the thinning out of the more densely populated permanent areas. This involved increasing the densities in the squatter areas by removing the existing shacks and replacing them with permanent three- or four-storey walk-up flats, supplemented with a small amount of row or terraced housing.

The new government's housing policy sought to broaden its involvement in housing by cooperating with private capital in the provision of housing and extending the government's activities to include middle-income groups in addition to low-income groups and slum clearance. One important stimulus to private development was the amendment to the Housing Act in 1958. This allowed the construction of private housing schemes operating under legal sanction and in some cases backed by government guarantee of mortgages. This initiative was essentially based on the recommendations of the 1952 committee chaired by the Government Town Planner and gave permission to private construction companies to develop housing schemes. As a result, a number of middle-income housing schemes were constructed with government providing the land at below market rates and also guaranteeing the mortgages and private companies financing

61

the construction costs. The first of these schemes, Mona Heights, was completed in 1958 with a selling price of US $6,000. This was followed by cheaper schemes at Pembroke Hall (US $3,600) and Harbour View (US $4,000) and the more expensive schemes at Trafalgar Park (US $9,000) and Hope Pastures (US $11,000) (Norton, 1978).

The availability of low-cost mortgage money for the construction of housing to meet the need of middle- and low-income earners was one of the key factors which gave birth to West Indies Home Contractors (WIHCON), the single largest developer and producer of mass housing communities and related social infrastructure in Jamaica. The company began operations in 1958 with the construction of Mona Heights, where houses were built mainly of reinforced concrete walls and roofs and strip footings. Although this system is no longer in use by the company today, it was this start that allowed WIHCON to develop a system uniquely suited to tropical regions where affordable housing is a priority (Matalon, 1996). At the start of the company, at the time of building Mona Heights, WICHON negotiated with the Commonwealth Development Corporation and Standard Life of Scotland for interim and mortgage financing for the project. This first venture set a pattern for the company which over the years has sought and negotiated the simultaneous provision of interim and mortgage financing for the majority of its developments (Matalon, 1996).

The change of government in 1955 also had an impact on town planning as the new government stressed the necessity for planned development, as a reflection of its socialist origins (Clarke, 1975). In 1957, the Town Planning Department was established within the portfolio of the Chief Minister and the Minister of Development and Welfare, with the objective of coordinating physical and socio-economic planning and the first Town and Country Planning Act came into operation (Mills, 1995). In the same year, the department prepared a series of maps to illustrate the ten year plan of 1957–67. Topics covered included population distribution, existing and proposed high schools and types of roads, but this programme made no mention of either regional or town planning (Clarke, 1975). At about the same time,

Robert Moses, Commissioner of the New York State Park, visited the country to advise on park development in the Palisadoes area (Mills, 1975). The Town Planning Department prepared the plans and organised the development of Gunboat Beach, a public park and beach area on the Palisadoes. The TPD was also involved in the preparation of a redevelopment plan for the town centre of Lucea, which was later implemented to a large degree.

In Kingston, planning activities were mainly concerned with the siting of the Washington Boulevard and the layout of government housing schemes. Through these housing schemes, the government was playing an important role in shaping the land use patterns in the capital city. Clarke (1975) has noted, however, that the initial intervention of the government was not a spontaneous response to the widespread need and the catalyst for action was provided by the hurricane of 1951.

Summary

The effectiveness of the 1957 Town and Country Act and how it has worked in practice will be discussed in Chapters III and IV. It may be useful, however, to point out a few important issues at this time. First, rapid expansion and suburbanisation was taking place in the city as land was subdivided to meet the city's demand for housing. It would appear that the local authorities under the Local Improvements Act were in charge of a subdivision process which regulated private developers. On the other hand, the Ministry of Housing and laterally the Town Planning Department played important roles in the provision of government housing. In effect, there were two systems in operation with very little coordination between them.

Second, the role which was continually assigned to the Town Planning Department during its formative years did not place the department in the mainstream of policy and decision making. Its early functions consisted of providing advice to the Ministry of Housing and preparing land use maps. Even when the department was assigned additional functions in 1957, no specific role was given to the department to prepare urban and regional policies and plans.

Third, the enactment of the Town and Country Planning Act in 1957 did not change significantly the role assigned to spatial planning. The Act was promulgated mainly in response to the problems arising from rapid urbanisation and expansion of the Kingston Metropolitan Area. It was designed specifically to control development in the city and other parts of the island which were experiencing urban growth. It established the means for applying development control regulations rather than promoting comprehensive development.

Fourth, the Local Improvements Act was not replaced by the comprehensive Town and Country Planning Act which governed all land use development activities. Both acts continued to operate side by side resulting also in different procedures and regulations governing land development in the country. Finally, although the Town and Country Planning Act was promulgated at about the same time that national development planning was being introduced into the country, these branches of planning evolved separately. Land development had its origins in the Local Improvements Act (subdivision) and the housing movement, both of which were introduced much earlier than national planning. This in part accounts for the separation of economic and spatial planning and juxtaposing them in the same ministry was not sufficient to bring them together.

Chapter III

STRUCTURE OF THE PLANNING SYSTEM

With the enactment of the Town and Country Planning Act in 1957 a clear distinction was made between development and subdivision (dividing land into smaller parcels that may be sold to others). The latter is governed by the Local Improvements Act, while development is defined under Section 5 (2) Town and Country Planning Act as follows:

> The carrying out of building, engineering, mining or any operations in, on, over or under land, or the making of any material change in the use of any building or other land.

Certain works or uses are specifically excluded from this definition. They include works of maintenance, improvement, or alteration which affect only the interior of a building, the use of the buildings or land within the curtilage of a dwelling house and where land or a building is used for a purpose within a class defined in the schedule of a development order. The definition of development (constructing buildings and/or other physical improvements and changing the use of land), as stated in the Town and Country Planning Act does not include the 'development' of raw land. In strict legal terms subdivision of land is not considered development. However, planning permission must be sought before land may be subdivided. Therefore, for development control purposes, i.e. applying for planning permission, subdivision is considered 'development'. Nonetheless, the legal basis for planning in Jamaica does not conform to and support the objective of one integrated and comprehensive system.

Because the land use regulatory framework is governed by two different acts, the procedures to apply for permission to subdivide and to develop land vary considerably as does development guidance. This separation influences the actions of all those involved in the approval process, including the government itself. Inadequate communication between the regulatory agencies at central government level, absence of planning coordination and inadequate institutional capability are the major problems affecting the development approval process. Thus, the development approval process is subject to the same problems which beset the subdivision approval process and which were discussed in the previous chapter. Remedial action as set out in Chapter II, namely, setting up a 'one-stop' approval system, also applies to the development approval process.

In this chapter we examine the 'planning system' – as it is convenient to call it – as the responsibility for guiding the development of land rests primarily with the Town and Country Planning Act. We will examine how the system has worked in practice and its effectiveness in promoting sustainable development in Jamaica. We also will examine the Urban Development Corporation Act and the Housing Act to determine the impact of these laws on the planning system and the objective of achieving one integrated system for spatial planning and development guidance. The usefulness of the Land Development and Duty Law as a capital gains and betterment tax will also be discussed.

The Planning System

The planning system focuses essentially on the orderly use of land. In this regard, the system operates through a process of strong negative controls. Good positive planning in the form of development projects is carried out by the central government ministries and their agencies, as we will see in Chapter IV. The negative powers of control are used mainly to regulate the activities of the private developer. The planning system is yet to recognise that the comprehensive planning and management of human settlements can contribute significantly to economic development. There is a need for greater coordination among the agencies involved in the planning and development of human settlements. The role of the Town Planning Department needs to be strengthened to develop an institutional framework that creates real coordination by working with the implementation agencies from the start of the planning process so that there is spatial coordination of public development programmes. There is a need to establish a mechanism for spatial coordination and review of sector projects and programmes. The current planning system relies on a centralised process and is essentially negative in its approach. The factors responsible for and the outcome of this approach will be discussed in the remainder of this chapter.

Development Orders

LEGAL BASIS OF DEVELOPMENT ORDERS

Development orders are the statutory instruments under the Town and Country Planning Act which control and regulate the use of land. A development order specifies the area to which it relates, gives directions as to how one may obtain planning permission and provides policies to guide development of land in the area specified. The Town and Country Planning Act provides for the creation of a Town and Country Planning Authority. Under Section 5 (1), this authority:

> May after consultation with the local authority concerned prepare so many or such provisional development orders as the Authority may consider necessary in relation to any land, in any urban or rural area, whether there are or are not buildings thereon, with the general objective of controlling the development of the land comprised in the area to which the respective order applies, and with a view to securing proper sanitary conditions and conveniences and the coordination of roads and public services, protecting and extending the amenities, and conserving and developing the resources, of such area.

As soon as a provisional development order is prepared, the authority must publish in the *Gazette* and a daily newspaper that the authority has prepared an order; the area to which the order applies; a place where the order can be viewed; the name and address of persons from whom the order may be obtained, and the fee involved. Once the period of objections has passed, the minister shall confirm the order with or without amendment.

Scope and Content

Section 10 of the Act states that a confirmed order is referred to as a development order and shall: specify and define clearly the area to which it relates; contain such provisions as are necessary or expedient for prohibiting or regulating the development of land in the area to which the development order applies and generally for carrying out any of the objects for which the order is made; provide for the grant of permission for the development of land in the area to which the development order applies. Certain classes of development are 'permitted development' i.e. they are given general permission by the development order and may be carried out without specific permission. These classes and the conditions attached to the general permission in respect of each class are defined in the development order.

The most important feature of the Act is that it created the development order. It did not ensure, however, effective public control over the development and use of land in accordance with a plan. The development order is, in effect, a zoning ordinance and like all zoning ordinances consists of two parts: a zoning map and a text of regulations. The map divides the area into functional zones; the text states how land may be used within each class of zone. Zones are designated by their predominant allowed use viz. residential, commercial, industrial etc. Restrictions on use are supplemented by rules on density and bulk. Density limits are established through minimum lot size requirements for residential use. The regulation of bulk takes the form of minimum front, side and rear yard dimensions and height limitations.

The Town and Country Planning Act created an instrument, the development order, which has strong negative connotations through its development control bias. There was no attempt to link plan making with development control through the preparation of a development plan for the area, based on survey and analysis. Such a plan would have consisted of a written statement and maps, showing all important developments and intended changes in the use of land over a twenty year future period. As a consequence, most development orders are no longer relevant to the current development trends and objectives of the parishes. The TPD has tried to overcome this problem in recent times by preparing a development plan on which the development order is based. The Town and Country Planning (St Ann Parish) Provisional Development Order, 1998 was prepared using this technique.

Under Section 11 (1) of the Town and Country Planning Act application for permission to develop land must be made to a local planning authority, in the case of the parishes of Kingston and St Andrew, the KSAC; to the parish council of any other parish; and in any area situated within two or more parishes, to the person or body that the minister may appoint. However, this procedure which ensures that the local authorities have some control over the development process in their parish is not guaranteed. Planning powers conferred on any local authority may be removed by the Town and Country Planning Authority (TCPA) by 'calling in' development under Section 12 of the Town and Country Planning Act which states:

> The Authority may give directions to any local planning authority requiring that any application for permission to develop land, or all such applications for permission to develop land, or all such applications of any class specified in the directions, shall be referred to the TCPA instead of being dealt with by the local planning authority.

This power has been used on many occasions by the TCPA, 'calling-in' development on the grounds that the local authority was approving development that did not conform to the development order for the area. This 'calling-in' mechanism often leads to problems of enforcement. Although the authority 'calls-in' development, enforcement remains the responsibility of the local authority, which in the circumstances tends to limit its activities.

A prerequisite for planning permission is that the site of the development order area in areas where there are no development orders permission for the erection of buildings fall under the Building Act (local building regulations), which is the responsibility of the parish councils. Generally, only small residential building applications are processed at a local level; all other development applications are received by the local planning authority, processed and sent to the Town and Country Planning Authority for further assessment and comments. This assessment is done by the Town Planning Department which acts as the technical secretariat to the Town and Country Planning Authority. Most local planning authorities have to adopt this procedure as they lack the skills and capacity to assess the planning implications of the larger developments. This leads to further centralisation of the process and limited involvement of the local authorities.

Permission for a development may be granted either conditionally or unconditionally or it may be refused. If the applicant is aggrieved by the decision handed down by the local planning authority or the Town and Country Planning Authority, he or she has the right to appeal to the minister (Section 13 of the Town and Country Planning Act) within twenty-eight days of the receipt of the decision.

Procedures for Application to Develop Land

There are seven types of application for development: application for determination of planning permission; outline planning application; full planning application; change of use application; retention of use application; application for advertisements and application for petrol filling stations. If a developer wants to know whether planning permission is needed prior to the commencement of a development he can apply for determination according to Section 14 of the Town and Country Planning Act. An inquiry may be made to the Town Planning Department or local planning authority. One copy of the application for determination must be submitted containing the following information: a description of the proposed operations or change of use; a description of the lands in which the operations will be carried out; the address of the property; a location plan of the property; and the area of the land.

Applications for permission to erect buildings may be made in outline, and permission may be given, subject to the local authorities' or Town and Country Planning Authority's approval of reserved matters such as siting, external appearance, access and design. This allows the developer to know if his proposal would be acceptable without preparing detailed plans which might involve abortive work. The granting of planning permission in respect of an outline application is not considered planning permission to build. No construction work may commence until approval of the reserved matters is given. In addition, building permission under the appropriate building law of the local authority concerned has to be granted before construction commences.

Full planning applications are those in which the developer, without any reservations, seeks outright planning approval for the proposed development. Two copies of the subdivision approval (if applicable), site layout plan, location plan, fully detailed drawings, landscaping plans and written details of the proposal and other relevant information are submitted to the parish council or the KSAC. As indicated earlier, the Town Planning Department as the advisory body is usually consulted if the proposal is for development other than a single family residence, for example, commercial, office, multi-storey or industrial development.

Under the Town and Country Planning Act, any material change of use of any building or land also requires planning permission. The second schedule of development orders contains a list of 'use classes' which stipulates the acceptable use in each class for which planning permission is not required. In applying for a change of use, the applicant should submit his documents and plans to the local planning authority. Documentation and information required for retention of use application are the same as for change of use except the applicant is required to have written details on the use to be retained.

The Town and Country Planning Act (Control of Advertisement) regulations of 1978 apply to the display of advertisements on all lands covered by development orders. Persons are required to apply for permission to advertise in such areas. Advertisements not complying with the conditions under which consent was granted are subject to enforcement procedures against which persons may appeal to the minister. Planning registers are kept by the local planning authorities. This is done in accordance with Part III, Section 2 – (4) of the Town and Country Planning Act which states:

> Every local planning authority shall keep in such manner as may
> be prescribed by the development order a register containing such
> information as to the manner in which such applications have
> been dealt with; and every register shall be available for inspection
> by the public at all reasonable hours.

Applicants may search the register to ascertain whether there has
been previous applications on the land they plan to develop and
how applications on adjoining lands may have been dealt with.
However, this facility is not often used.

Conflicts within the Planning System

In addition to the complex procedures required for development
control purposes, the enactment of the NRCA Act (1991) has
given rise to the possibility of conflict between that Act and the
Town and Country Planning Act. Section 33 of the NRCA Act
(1991) empowers the relevant Minister to declare special areas,
regulating development activities in said areas. This would create
some ambiguity in terms of responsibility for regulating development activities in areas covered by development orders, unless
mechanisms are developed for consultation and coordination.

Another area of concern is the increased cost of development.
With the introduction of the environmental permit and licensing
system in 1997, the Natural Resources Conservation Authority
(NRCA) is authorised under the NRCA Act to issue permits for
development projects (including subdivisions of ten lots or more).
Costs associated with land regulation include direct costs in terms
of fees and costs in time and manpower to obtain the necessary
papers and permits. The developer and householder is now
required to pay two sets of fees for the same application. In this
regard, it should be noted that under the local government reform
process greater autonomy has been granted to parish councils and
the KSAC in the setting and adjustment of licence fees and user
fees in respect of the services and regulatory functions for which
the councils are responsible. This has resulted in increases to most
existing licence and user charges. Building and subdivision fees
now contribute the largest percentage share of locally collected

revenue (McHardy, 1999). The process for obtaining approval from the local authority is tedious and the system has not improved significantly despite the increase in fees. One can assume that the costly delays experienced in the approval system will increase with the additional procedures and permits now required from both the local authorities and the NRCA.

Coverage of Development Orders

According to the Town and Country Planning Act all development should conform with the zoning regulations set out in development orders. However, the entire island is not covered by such orders and therefore large portions of the island do not fall under the regulations of the Town and Country Planning Act. Coastal development orders have been prepared extending from the coast to about 1.6 kilometres inland from the main road for nearly the entire island. In addition, development orders have also been prepared for parish capitals and fast growing urban centres. The process of bringing the entire island under the purview of the Town and Country Planning Act has been very slow. This has resulted in different pieces of legislation governing various parts of the country and some confusion regarding development standards and procedures. In addition, in areas where the pressure for development is great problems related to limited development control such as the conversion of good agricultural land to residential and commercial use often arise.

Special mention must be made of the Negril Green Island Development Order, 1959 which was the first such Order to be promulgated. This development order encompasses the two parishes of Westmoreland (Negril) and Hanover (Green Island). Promulgation of a regional order was necessary because the area concerned represented unique criteria in terms of its development potential. Negril has been transformed from a fishing village into a major tourism destination based on a stretch of white sand beaches approximately twelve kilometres in length. The preparation of a development order was part of a strategy to develop the area as a coherent whole. Without this approach the area would have been assigned to two local authorities and this might have introduced inconsistencies in the development control process, as it was at this time that development in Negril commenced.

Another initiative undertaken was the appointment of the Negril Green Island Area Land Authority as the local planning authority. In fact, Section 11 (1) of the Town and Country Planning Act which states, *'in relation to any area situated within two or more parishes the person or body that the Minister in writing may appoint,'* was created specifically to accommodate Negril. However, the creation of this special planning authority has not achieved the desired aims, as will be discussed in Chapter IV.

In addition to the entire island not being covered by one set of rules and regulations regarding land use activities, most development orders are more than thirty years old. For example the St Catherine Coast Confirmed Development Order dates back to 1964, and the Clarendon Confirmed Development Order was prepared one year later in 1965. In 1981, the Negril Green Island Development Order was updated, and this provisional order was confirmed in 1984. Since then only one development order has been prepared, the Town and Country Planning (St Ann Parish) Provisional Development Order, 1998. Because development orders are basically outdated in many urban and rapidly urbanising areas it has become difficult to exercise effective control over development in these areas. The issues that arise as a result of this lack of control are squatting on government owned land or land reserved for open space; non-conforming uses; and land designated for particular uses in the development order have not been used for those purposes.

Until very recently (1998), development orders were very general documents with not even the major land use classes divided into sub-classes. In addition, because so many of the development orders were prepared so long ago they bear no relevance to the situation on the ground. Therefore, as a tool for guiding growth they have not been very effective. A clear example is the Kingston Development Order, which was prepared in 1966

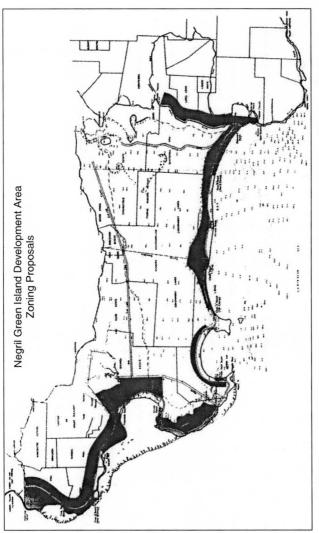

Negril Green Island Development Area
Zoning Proposals

Figure 3.1: Zoning proposals as set out in the Town and Country (Negril and Green Island area) Provisional Development Order (confirmation) notification, 1959. The order was the first development order prepared under the 1957 Town and Country Planning Act.

and still controls development in the Kingston Metropolitan Area. The preparation of this order was not based on realistic appraisals of the city's economic potential or likely population growth. The result is that there are competing uses for land, without an up-to-date instrument to guide and direct growth. Citizens living in the 'zone of transition' feel that their rights have been infringed when they see their residential property values falling because of the illegal encroachment of commercial and industrial activities onto their neighbourhoods.

The TPD has begun to address this problem by using the development plan to guide the preparation of the development order. While development plans have no legal status under the Town and Country Planning Act, the TPD prepared several development plans in the 1970s. The preparation of these plans slowed down considerably in the 1980s as the TPD was beset with staffing problems. Between 1991 and 1993, the TPD received assistance from the United Nations Development Programme which resulted in the preparation of four development plans. The development order for the parish of St Ann was the outcome of one of these development plans. However, the process has not been responsive to the real timing requirements of policy makers. It took almost five years from the completion of the development plan (1993) by the TPD to the promulgation of the St Ann Parish Provisional Development Order (1998) by the TCPA. Five years for the promulgation of a provisional development order is far too long.

There are several factors which account for the current status of development orders. First, their preparation is a highly centralised process and thus a lengthy one. The Town and Country Planning Act states that the TCPA may consult with the local authority concerned in the preparation of development orders. While a certain level of consultation takes place during the preparation process, it is the Town Planning Department, acting on behalf of the TCPA, which usually initiates the process. Because of the phraseology of the Act both the TCPA and the local authorities view the residual power for preparation of development orders to be residing with the TCPA. The Act does not empower the local authorities to take the proactive position of

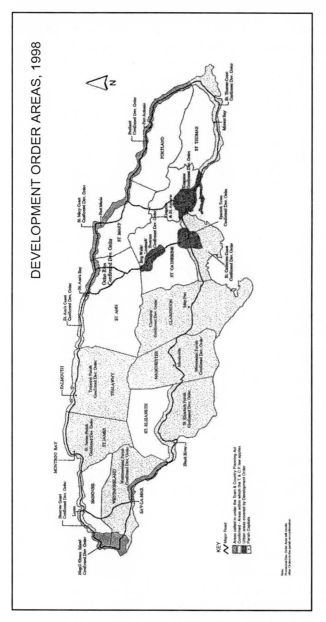

Figure 3.2: Areas of the island covered by development orders under the Town and Country Planning Act. NB A provisional order was completed for the parish of St Ann in 1998 and confirmed in 1999.

shaping the future of their own communities. In such a situation there tends to be inaction on both the side of the TCPA and that of the local authority, as neither body has accepted ownership for the process.

Second, development orders are not regularly updated and their static nature cannot keep up with the dynamic process of urban growth in Jamaica's towns and cities. The slow pace of preparation of development plans means that there is very little updating of development orders. In addition, because the development plan is not a legal document under the Town and Country Planning Act it has very little status as an instrument for guiding growth and development. The preparation of a development order should not be the only outcome of the development plan. There is a need to recognise the development plan as a tool for strengthening urban management, improving institutional coordination and creating stronger linkages between planning and implementation. The development plan should be more than a background document for preparing a development order as it addresses a wider range of public concerns other than land use. There is an urgent need to overcome institutional fragmentation in the planning and delivery of goods and services. Planning can no longer be separated from management and the plan should be used as the means through which the growth of towns and cities are properly managed.

The position assigned to spatial planning, vis-à-vis national (economic) planning, is another factor responsible for the current state of affairs with regard to development orders. National planning based on sector objectives is often pursued to the detriment of spatial planning. Local development objectives, constraints and possibilities are not usually considered or are given minor recognition in the pursuit of sector goals. Even where development plans have been prepared precedence is given to sector planning objectives. So, the development plan is ignored not only because it is seen as a background document for development orders, but also because central government agencies operations are based largely on pursuing sector objectives. Local authorities are generally unaware of the planning which takes place at a national level or within specific agencies and are usually consulted only during the implementation phase of the project. In this kind of environment development plans and orders are not seen as being particularly relevant to the development activities being pursued by government ministries and agencies.

ENFORCEMENT

Enforcement of planning control is the responsibility of the local planning authority. Prior to 1993, an enforcement notice could only be served by the local planning authority. However, in that year the Town and Country Planning Act was amended and section 23 (1) of the Act states that if it appears to the local planning authority, Government Town Planner or the TCPA that development has been carried out without, or contrary to, planning permission, then the various authorities may, within five years serve an enforcement notice. The law requires that the notice specifies the development alleged to have been carried out without permission, or the conditions which have not been complied with, and the action to correct the non-conforming development. The legislation also provides for the local authority to take the steps outlined in the notice which could include demolition, if the developer is reluctant to do so, and to recover the debt as an expense in a Resident Magistrate's Court. If the individual feels aggrieved by the serving of an enforcement notice he or she may appeal to a tribunal established for this purpose within twenty-eight days of the service of the notice. If the individual is not satisfied with the decision of the tribunal he or she may appeal to the Court of Appeal against that decision.

With the 1993 amendments to the Town and Country Planning Act several local planning authorities have been serving enforcement notices for various breaches committed under the Act. However, a number of problems have arisen consequent to the serving of enforcement notices. The major problems are: notices are not properly served by the local planning authority; notices are not explicit regarding the breach; there is a lack of follow-up action by the local planning authority to ensure that work does not resume prior to the determination of the appeal; the time period stipulated in the notice to pursue further action as permitted by the law is not observed by the local planning authority; and there are delays on the part of the courts in dealing with cases.

In 1999 there were further amendments to the Town and Country Planning Act in response to the growing concerns among the local authorities and citizens, due to the escalation of non-conforming uses in residential areas. The major reforms include the appeal tribunal being disbanded and the introduction of new enforcement measures, including stop orders, enforcement notices and injunctions. Local planning authorities may now obtain injunctions of non-conforming or illegal developments without having to go through the Attorney General's Department. Stop orders may now be served by the local planning authority to prohibit the carrying out of the activity to which the enforcement notice relates, before the expiry of the period for compliance with the enforcement notice. Enforcement notices are now more specific regarding the date on which they take effect and the time period for the required steps to take effect. These amendments to the Town and Country Planning Act should enable the local authorities to take faster action against violators and to have a logical series of notices served on non-conforming developments through the issuing of stop orders, enforcement notices and injunctions.

With regard to the process of hearing appeals one must view with concern the power given to the minister in the determination of illegal and non-conforming uses. The 1993 amendment of the Act allowed for the establishment of an appeal tribunal, and set out the constitution and procedures of the tribunal in the fourth schedule of the Act. The schedule clearly indicated that the tribunal should be made up of six members, two of whom should be attorneys-at-law and would be the chairman and vice chairman. The other members had to be competent in town and country planning matters. The appeal tribunal thus constituted could contribute a high level of expertise and by establishing rules to regulate its proceedings could be viewed almost as a body with some legal trappings. With the 1999 amendment to the Act the minister is empowered to hear appeals. The perception is that the independence of the appeal process has been compromised.

Although this may not be so in reality and the minister may appoint a committee to hear appeals, the fact that this is an ad hoc committee without specific guidelines regarding its constitution and procedures has not reduced the misgivings about the appeal process. Great care will have to be exercised in appointing commissioners to a committee and setting out the procedures of how the committee should operate.

Standards for Subdivision and Development

Under the Local Improvements Act local authorities are authorised to promulgate regulations, but they have never done so, at least not in a manner that specifies standards for evaluating applications. Standards governing development are supposed to be provided in confirmed development orders. However, except for the recently prepared St Ann Parish Order, most orders do not specify criteria in much detail. As a result, there was very little uniformity in the standards used to evaluate land subdivision and development. These standards varied among the various bodies approving these developments and developers were basically unaware of the requirements of the approving authorities. The lack of written standards available to all the stakeholders and the need to promote uniformity and a level of proficiency in development and subdivision standards led to the establishment in 1973 of a committee to study the matter. The committee involved the participation of the United Nations Development Programme which had just completed a National Physical Plan for Jamaica from 1970–90. Other members of the committee were the Town Planning Department, the Advisory Planning Committee and the Town and Country Planning Authority. In August 1973 the committee published *A Manual for Development* as a provisional document.

This provisional document offered guidance to architects, planners, engineers, land surveyors, developers and the general public and had the effect of providing written advice on standards for land subdivision and building for the first time. Through the information provided in the provisional manual the various approval agencies, professionals and developers involved in the development of land were assisted in achieving the coordination of activity needed to expedite the approval process.

STANDARDS REVIEW PROCEDURES AND PROCESSES

Updating the Manual for Development

The experience gained through the publication of the provisional work was used by the Town Planning Department in 1982 to update the document and to publish *A Manual for Development* in October, 1982. The Town Planning Department was assisted in the preparation of the manual by a committee made up of a varied group of individuals and organisations, including the Town and Country Planning Authority, the Advisory Planning Committee, the Jamaica Institute of Engineers, the Jamaica Institute of Architects, developers and other stakeholders in the development process.

Development standards stipulated in the manual have been used as a guide to project design by architects, engineers, planners, land surveyors, developers and others. As was indicated earlier the manual has no legal basis in law and therefore conformity to the provisions of the manual does not exempt a developer from any legal requirement or obligation stipulated in the Town and Country Planning Act, the Local Improvements Act, or any other Act pertaining to development. For example, standards presented in development orders are also applied in evaluating subdivision applications. In this regard, density schedules in the Kingston Development Order are applied to determine the acceptability of applications from that jurisdiction. Yet, other criteria used in the evaluation are not available in written form. These include criteria applied by outside referral agencies. The manual recommended therefore, that before acquiring land for development or preparing plans and drawings, the developer should seek professional guidance in respect of the laws, regulations and the planning instruments relating to the various aspects of the proposal. Such guidance could be obtained from the Town Planning Department or the local planning authorities. The committee that prepared the 1982 manual for development did not put in place any review procedures and the manual stated that *'revision of this document will be determined as deemed necessary'*.

Town Planning Review

In 1986 a project to review the operations of the Town Planning Department and to help devise recommendations for improvement was initiated. Phase I of the project was completed in 1987 and Phase II was completed in 1989. The project was funded by the United States of America's AID and implemented by the Urban Institute, operating out of Washington DC. The Phase II agenda included five tasks of which two addressed the issue of revising standards for buildings and the subdivision of land. The tasks which were given priority were: further improvement of TPD internal applications processing systems and streamlining reviews by external agencies; clarification and proposed improvements to Jamaica's subdivision and land development laws, regulations and standards.

Phase I of the project concluded that standards were often unclear and/or economically unrealistic and cumbersome. Phase I of the project examined the TPD's proposed development order for Kingston and St Andrew and found that the standards suggested were unrealistically high. Cost analyses of several development options showed that even a very modest house built to conform to the proposed standards would be unaffordable to all but the top 15% of the income distribution.

In its examination of development orders, the review committee recognised that problems with land subdivision and development standards in Jamaica were much more pervasive than those found in the text of the document. Anecdotal evidence suggested to the committee that at least some of the standards used in evaluating subdivision and development applications were not written and/or not made available to developers. Those that were written were fragmented (appearing in a number of different documents) and often not clearly specified.

Accordingly, the Phase II work programme entailed: the examination of all written documents concerning standards (laws, regulations, policy statements and internal guidelines); interviews about criteria used in evaluating applications with those who administer them and those who are affected by them (the applicants); further analysis of costs to identify those standards that have the largest effect on affordability; and an analysis of alternative approaches for designing more cost-effective subdivision and development standards for Jamaica. In order to accomplish this task, the consultants worked with a Standards Subcommittee of the Town Planning Department Review Committee and the Jamaica Institution of Engineers to draft a new manual for development as the central statement of proposed standards. The Subcommittee made the following recommendations (Kingsley et al, 1989).

Techniques of Efficient Site Planning

Because of increasing concerns reaching affordability, new site-planning techniques which permit notable cost reductions without commensurate losses in quality were recommended. A major change suggested was the use of zero-lot-line and row houses approaches which would have the effect of reducing the waste of space in residential lots in small unusable side lots. Thus it would be possible to use smaller plots without any real reduction in 'useable' outdoor space.

Cluster Approach

The 'conventional' design contains large lots that are all the same size. In contrast, the 'balanced' neighbourhood design offers the following advantages that would be relevant for site design in Jamaica:

257%	more common open space
16%	smaller average lot size
9%	less linear feet of roads
37%	less road surface (sq ft)
19%	less lineal feet of water drains
53%	less lineal feet of storm sewer
33%	less total cost of land and infrastructure

Cost Effects of Alternative Designs

To test further the effects of alternative standards in Jamaica, the Subcommittee developed optional plans for a site which was the subject of a subdivision application pending at the Town Planning Department. These options are set out in Table I. Option 1 entailed large lots, averaging 4,091 sq ft, roughly the minimum size that can utilise site sanitation options according to present standards, and provides a total of twenty-six lots. The lots in option 2 averaged 1,510 sq ft, and the total number is seventy-six. Option 2 also takes advantage of the cluster approach, which permits narrower roads into cul-de-sacs and fewer lineal feet of road and water or sewerage pipe. As would be expected, given its higher density, the total cost of a serviced lot in option 2 is much lower than for option 1: $34,467 and $72,879 (prices at the time the study was completed), respectively (Kingsley et al, 1989).

Reduction of Lot Sizes

Based on their analysis the Subcommittee recommended that the minimum lot size should be around 1,500 sq ft, where soil conditions are appropriate. Aside from the cost argument, the Subcommittee felt that there were good design reasons for reducing such excessive requirements for suburban areas and cities and towns outside of metropolitan Kingston. Large minimum lot sizes create uniformity and sterility in site planning. Mixtures, including some areas of fairly high-density development, are necessary to create visual interest as well as achieve the social objectives of some mixing of income groups.

Table I: *Structure of Land and Site Development Costs in 1989*

	Option 1 (4,091 sq ft)		Option 2 (1,510 sq ft)	
	J $/lot	%	J $/lot	%
Land cost	21,002	28.8	8,403	24.4
Infrastructure				
Roads	12,265	16.8	3,556	10.3
Walkways	6,393	7.4	2,193	6.4
Water supply	6,097	7.0	2,230	6.5
Sanitation collection	8,758	12.0	4,240	12.3
Sanitation treatment	18,960	26.0	12,957	37.6
Storm drainage	1,154	1.6	658	1.9
Subtotal	51,627	70.8	25,834	75.0
Landscaping	230	0.3	230	07
TOTAL	72,879	100.0	34,467	100.0

Source: *Improving Jamaica's Land Regulations and Processing Systems*, Kingsley et al, 1989, p.41.

Affordable Standards for Subdivision and Development

The TPD Review Committee concluded that many of the standards and procedures used were inherited at the time of independence and were further extended by the extremely cautious attitudes of professionals in the 1960s and 1970s with respect to health hazards. Sizeable 'safety factors' were added without regard for their impact on development. The urban land use ratio in metropolitan Kingston (48 acres per 1,000 inhabitants) exceeds the average for many large cities in the United States of America and is about 2.5 times the average for developing countries (Kingsley et al, 1989). The review committee pointed out that unless this level of land waste is reduced in relation to the economy, there will be clearly unacceptable urban encroachment into prime agricultural lands and environmentally sensitive areas as cities grow. In addition, decent infrastructure will be unaffordable (excessive urban land use implies excessive lengths for streets and water and sanitation networks) and most new urban households will be forced to build crude shelters illegally on land which they illegally occupy (Kingsley et al, 1989).

Preparation of a New Manual for Development

The subcommittee recommended the promulgation of a new *Manual for Development* for the evaluation of subdivisions and the planning aspects of development applications. The TPD Review Committee pointed out that analysis in Phase II showed that due to the lack of any clear written standards in several areas, no one has a clear definition of all of the criteria by which applications will either be accepted or rejected. The committee further recommended that as the *Manual for Development* is the most comprehensive statement it should be revised as needed to: make the document generally more readable; modify existing standards so that they are economically realistic and add standards in areas where rules are not clear.

What may be considered to be the first major review of development standards for low-income housing was that completed in 1987. This review was conducted with the view that the subdivision and development regulations were rigid, in may respects unclear and economically unrealistic. In addition, many of the agencies to which applications were referred for review by the Town Planning Department had no written standards to guide their decisions and nothing to guide developers as to the criteria according to which their applications would be evaluated. Those that were written were fragmented (appearing in a number of different documents) and often not clearly specified. In this regard a recommendation of the 1987 Review Committee was as follows:

> A major objective for Jamaica's land development guidance system should be the creation of one clear and internally consistent presentation of all applicable land development regulations.

In March 1993, a draft development manual was produced by a consultant to the government's administrative reform programme. This first edition was for the purpose of generating discussion and input from all relevant groups, public and private. The document contained certain sections that were simply a redefinition of sections contained in the 1982 development manual. Substantially the document is aimed at major changes in procedures and systems, and re-values various responsibilities and tasks in the approval process which were implemented as part of the Town Planning Review Project mentioned earlier. The aims and objectives of the document were to assist in the implementation of the planning reforms which are underway at the Town Planning Department. The introduction to the revised manual, unlike the 1982 manual, states that it is essential that publications such as the manual remain under constant review and examination, in order to ensure that their contents represent emerging attitudes and directions in the complex area of development. In this regard, therefore, it was the Town Planning Department's intention to pursue and implement reviews as it becomes evident that community standards demand change, and such changes will always reflect corresponding reforms in regulations and planning procedures.

The revised manual has been circulated to the local authorities for their comments. This represents one of major hold-ups in finalising the document as, to date, not many of these agencies have forwarded their comments to the then Government Town

Planner. Another hold-up in finalising and releasing the manual as a policy document relates to changes in the Town and Country Planning Act. A new Act has been drafted, one which includes the definition of subdivision as development, thus removing the need for two acts in the development approval process.

Minimum Standards for Housing Development

In the interim, however, the alarming growth of informal settlements in all major towns and cities in Jamaica has become more prevalent since the 1980s with accelerating urbanisation. It is felt that this growth of squatter settlements is due in large measure to unaffordable high standards as these standards are a major constraint to the efficient delivery of affordable housing. In addition, the severe economic conditions being experienced by the country in the 1980s dictated that considerably more attention be paid to development costs. Therefore, following the advice of the TPD Review Committee and the Standards Review Subcommittee, the Town Planning Department in March 1992 produced a document entitled *Proposal for the Introduction of Minimum Standards for Housing Development and Upgrading Low-Income Areas in Jamaica*. The objective of the document was to formulate a set of realistic minimum standards which could be applied to the shelter related activities of the lower-income groups in Jamaica.

The standards were set against the prevailing circumstances which were having an impact on the low-income housing delivery process and the urgent need to address the issue before the promulgation of the new Town and Country Planning Act. The standards proposed by the TPD in 1992 were developed therefore as a guide for further discussion and consultation in the process of producing a working document which could be used to guide housing development in low-income areas. In this regard, most of the standards were based on information obtained from the agencies involved in sites and services projects. The document was not an attempt to undertake a detailed review of all aspects of standard-making associated with low-income housing development, as the issue of building codes was not addressed. Rather, it looked at those issues which formed part of the 1987 review: site design, plot development standards, amenities and infrastructure.

However, the document was never circulated and the government-led process of preparing minimal standards came to an end without any real action.

In 1993, the issue was taken up by a non-governmental organisation known as ASCEND. The Association for Settlement and Commercial Enterprise for National Development emerged in 1993 and was legally registered in 1994 as a non profit-making company. The mission of ASCEND is to assist in formulating policies and programmes to deal with the establishment of safe and legal low-income settlements and to reduce the exposure of low-income families to environmental health risks and natural hazards of settlements established by squatting, by encouraging holistic development and regularisation of areas where feasible. ASCEND has forged links with the government's 'Operation Pride' – Programme for Resettlement and Integrated Development Enterprise – a programme designed to make more land available to a wide range of persons, including squatters, for a variety of uses, but mainly residential.

ASCEND is a national coalition of the private, public and non-governmental sectors including professional bodies. In its efforts to encourage holistic development five Subcommittees have been established to deal with what the organisation sees as five critical areas. These committees are: (a) physical planning and development; (b) legal and public education; (c) quality of life; (d) economic and financial; and (e) communications. These Subcommittees are the policy-making arm of ASCEND and are responsible for developing proposals which will put its strategies into operation. This takes the form of policies or manuals which ASCEND had anticipated would be revised based on feedback in the implementation process.

To date, ASCEND has produced the *Starter Standards Manual, Community Development Manual, Affordable House Types Manual, Beneficiaries Policy Manual* and *Beneficiary Selection Policies Manual.* The preparation of these manuals was funded by local agencies and USAID. The *Starter Standards Manual* attempts to reform those standards that have the greatest impact on affordability namely: lot sizes, residential densities, setbacks, plot coverage, open space, water and sanitation standards and road widths and

89

surfacing. A separate, though related, guide has been developed with specific reference to shelter units. A manual of more than sixty small house designs for persons wishing to build their own homes has been prepared.

However, for the standard review process to be effective it must *involve all the stakeholders* at the planning stage, including the local authorities, developers and the agencies to which development applications are made. All criteria used in the assessment process should be discussed and decisions taken on how these standards should be incorporated and updated as part of the process. Foremost among the stakeholders are the local authorities. With regard to the *Manual for Development*, the 1987 Standards Review Committee pointed out that there are a number of unwritten criteria and guidelines used by the local authorities which should be discussed and brought into the process but these still have not been included in the 1993 development manual. The fact that one of the hold-ups in finalising the 1993 manual has been the slow response from local authorities in providing comments on the manual relates in large measure to their limited involvement in the process.

Information on standards must be *disseminated to all stakeholders*. There is a general lack of awareness of the consumers, particularly among low-income groups, as to where to obtain information if they want it. In addition the information is not in a readily accessible form. There is also need for improved communication between central government and local government on planning matters and the publication of brochures and guidelines for dissemination to the public through the local authorities. Central government must organise workshops and training sessions to assist local government personnel in understanding revised standards and the reasons behind their promulgation.

There is need also for *clear review institutions and procedures and schedules* to ensure clarity on who spearheads and who should participate in the review process.

The Housing Act and Planning

While concern over housing conditions in the country led in part to the establishment of the planning system there are areas of conflict between the Housing Act and the Town and Country Planning Act. In 1966 the Department of Housing was reorganised into the Ministry of Housing and the Housing Act was once again amended in 1968. The Act now gave power to the Minister of Housing to own land and established a revolving fund for housing which allowed money collected from mortgages to be paid into a housing fund thus bypassing the consolidated fund.

The intention of the Housing Act (1968) is to facilitate the development of housing by giving the minister the right to make a site-specific development plan for lands vested in him. These lands must be declared as housing areas, and the plans must be submitted to the local authorities for comment prior to being approved by the minister. However, the development need not conform to the standards established by the local authorities in order to be approved by the minister under the provisions of the Housing Act. In addition, the minister does not have to take into consideration the comments of the local authorities in approving the scheme under the Act, although he must afford the local authority an opportunity to be heard and make such objections or representations.

Most local authorities feel aggrieved when housing developments over which they have no control are approved for their parish. Although under the Housing Act the local authority should be informed of the scheme this often does not happen. Even if they are informed the councils rarely object as there is the perception that their representations go unheeded. One of the most grievous concerns of the local authorities are the standards used in the development, particularly as they relate to roads in the scheme. Under Section 28 of the Act the minister is empowered to vest control and management of all roads in the scheme in the appropriate local authority as they are now deemed parochial roads in accordance with Section 4 of the Parochial Roads Law. This is often a source of conflict between central government and local government, as councils complain that they are handed these roads without adequate notice and resources to maintain them.

Of greater concern, however, is the promotion of minimal standards in sites and services schemes. When roads are not

91

constructed to prescribed standards the local authorities often refuse to take over responsibility of these roads for maintenance purposes. The standards set for roads by the local authorities are twenty foot carriageways with twenty foot reservations and typical spray and chip finish, except where steep slopes indicate high erosion, then barber greene is required as well. In the past there have been problems in getting local authorities to approve resettlement schemes in bauxite areas because not all the services provided were to the standards set by the councils (McHardy, 1997b). In these circumstances the pre-checked plan cannot be submitted for approval to the Survey Department and titles cannot be issued. This has serious implications for the use of starter standards in sites and services schemes which promote on-lot sewerage and minimal provision of roads. All this points to the need for greater participation of the local authorities at every level of the planning system.

The Housing Act (1968) has not only generated conflict between central and local governments, but has also generated conflict between the Ministry of Housing and the Town Planning Department, both central government departments. Under Section 47 of the Housing Act (1968), a housing association may prepare and submit to the minister a scheme for the laying out or subdivision of land and the construction of houses. A housing association is any person, company, or society involved in the construction of houses and has been certified as a housing association by the minister. Such schemes may be approved by the local authorities or parliament. The latter route is the one normally used to approve such schemes. When this route is used for approval the housing association is exempt from any obligation imposed by law in relation to:

(i) the laying out or subdividing of land for the purpose of building thereon or for the selling of the same in lots; or
(ii) the construction of buildings

Section 49 2(a) Housing Act

The TPD complains that schemes approved in this way are not subject to the same review process as those approved for private developers and the Act should be amended to bind the Crown. The contention being that schemes not subject to review usually end up being thwart with problems, such as flooding or inadequate water supply. The Ministry of Housing on the other hand complains that the review process is too time consuming. However, the answer does not lie in the removal of schemes from the review process but rather in the reform of the planning system. With the introduction of the environmental permit and licensing system in 1997, the NRCA Act (1991) does bind the Crown to some extent as permits must be issued for development projects (including subdivisions of ten lots or more), although such projects do not undergo the TPD review process.

Urban Development Corporation Act

The Urban Development Corporation (UDC) Act (1968), like the Housing Act gives the UDC the right to make site-specific development plans for land which is designated under the Act. The UDC shall as soon as practicable after a designation order has been made, furnish every local authority within whose area the relevant designated area or part thereof is situated with a plan for development. The plan together with the comments of the local authority are then forwarded to the relevant minister for his approval. Like the review process under the Housing Act, the minister does not have to take the comments of the local authority into consideration.

The UDC Act gives the corporation power to sell or lease any land vested in the corporation. The corporation is responsible for the laying out and development of its designated areas and as such the corporation is also exempt from any obligation imposed by any law in relation to:

(i) the laying out or subdividing of land for the purpose of building thereon or for the selling of the same in lots; or
(ii) the construction of buildings

Section 21 (2) UDC Act

The corporation may for the purposes of an approved plan of

development:

> (i) lay out, pave, improve, sewer and complete such roads as it thinks fit within the designated area to which the plan relates;
> (ii) close, alter or discontinue any road within such area.

Section 22 (1) UDC Act

In effect, the UDC operates as a local planning authority and a developer within its designated area which sometimes leads to conflicts when designated areas fall within development order areas. In many instances the UDC does not have to conform to the density and other standards as set out in development orders when undertaking development in their designated areas.

LAND DEVELOPMENT DUTY ACT

The Land Development and Duty Act was introduced in 1958 as a type of capital gains and betterment tax. The Act was designed primarily as a result of the development taking place in Negril. The purpose of the Act was to enable the government and the public to recoup some of the value accruing to private land as a result of major roadways and other public improvement investment (Mills, 1995). It was intended that the money collected would have been spent on the purchase of land needed for the development of Negril. However, this never happened because land ownership in the area was problematic. Landowners whose land bordered on the swamps were required to pay betterment taxes on this land, but the largest landowner in the area refused, a decision he later regretted as, when he tried to claim the land, he was refused on the grounds of non-payment of taxes (McKay, 1987). Moreover, when a survey map of the area was prepared in 1962, it revealed that very few landowners held titles to the land as it was largely family land. Collecting the betterment tax therefore proved difficult and the Act has not been used since.

Summary

The planning system in Jamaica is complex and based on outdated and inappropriate legislation that still hangs on to the colonial

An example of the complications of land betterment [handwritten marginal note]

past. The system is made even more complex by having two acts which govern the development of land. With the enactment of the Town and Country Planning Act in 1957, the Local Improvements Act was not repealed or amended. The result is that the rules and procedures which govern subdivision and development vary considerably.

The planning system is also ambiguous about the real role assigned to the local authorities. Although the local authorities are responsible for granting permission to subdivide land the real power for approving of refusing a subdivision application rests with the Government Town Planner and the relevant minister. All subdivisions, by law, must be referred to the GTP for an opinion. This recommendation cannot be refused by the local authorities without first explaining to the GTP the reason for refusing the recommendation. In addition, the entire subdivision referral process has been instituted by the Town Planning Department although this is not a legal requirement. While there is much to be gained from having other agencies comment on large subdivisions, the process has become tortuous. Remedies proposed to untangle the approval process and reduce processing time point to further centralisation of the process on the one hand and further alienation of the local authorities on the other. With regard to development, local authorities can have the power to act as a local planning authority removed if the Town and Country Planning Authority 'calls in' development in their parish. The TCPA then assumes the role of the local planning authority, by granting or refusing permission to develop land.

Since the enactment of the Town and Country Planning Act in 1957, large portions of the island still have not been brought under the purview of the Act as development orders have not been prepared for the entire island. In addition, most of these development orders are at least thirty years old and no longer relevant as instruments with which to guide growth and development. To complicate the issue even further the preparation and enforcement of development orders are based on obsolete planning ordinances that place all the planning responsibilities with central government but enforcement with the local planning authority. While recent amendments to the

Town and Country Planning Act allow central government to serve enforcement notices, the executive system for enforcement still rests with the local authority. This situation has resulted in a wide gap between the preparation and enforcement of development orders and no clear understanding on the part of the local authorities that they are responsible for enforcement.

Institutional fragmentation in the land development process has contributed to the isolation of the planning function and its lack of coordination with the work of the infrastructure delivery agencies. There is also the problem that both the Minister of Housing and the UDC can subdivide and develop land under their respective acts without reference to the Town and Country Planning Act as the latter Act does not bind the Crown. This has added to the difficulties of collaboration and coordination experienced within the planning system.

Although several amendments have been made to the Town and Country Planning Act since its promulgation in 1957, the basic structure of the Act remains intact. In this regard, therefore, other responses have been put forward to deal with the problems of urbanisation rather than making major adjustments to the Act. For example, the UDC Act (1968) and the Urban Development Corporation were established to deal with the problem of urban renewal in the capital city, Kingston and to stimulate development activities in other towns. Rather than setting up a development corporation under the aegis of the Town and Country Planning Act, the UDC Act when passed into law made the new corporation not only responsible for construction activities but also a local planning authority in its designated areas. This has resulted in the untenable situation where two sets of development standards operate in the same general area, with the stricter standards usually directed towards the private developer.

maintains the 1957Act.

Chapter IV

URBAN DEVELOPMENT AND REDEVELOPMENT

In Chapters II and III we outlined the legal mechanisms which gave rise to the planning system as it exists in Jamaica today. At the core of this system is the Town and Country Planning Act of 1957. We also saw that this Act and thus the main focus of the system is to control and regulate the pace and direction of changes with regard to land use. The main argument for the introduction of the 1957 Act was to reduce the opposition to the planned use of land and orderly urban development in the public interest as this had frustrated plans to solve problems of urbanisation throughout the region (Hudson, 1980). Thus, we find the then prime minister when introducing the law in 1957 observed that:

> 'the enlightened landowners themselves are the first to see the necessity of the law.' The Jamaican leader went on to refer to planning in Puerto Rico, where, he said, 'I find that it is the owners of the land who find the law to their benefit, and will find property-value enhanced by an orderly instead of a haphazard manner of development.

> (cited in Hudson, 1980, p.12)

The system was designed essentially to regulate private developers, and, as we saw in Chapter III, from the very outset it was stronger in terms of its negative powers rather than initiating positive change. At the same time the bulk of urban development and redevelopment was carried out by government ministries and agencies. As was also indicated in Chapter III, legislation enacted after the Town and Country Planning Act empowered the Minister of Housing and the UDC to carry out land development activities without reference to the 1957 Act. The government agencies, themselves, sometimes undertake development schemes which are contrary to the plans prepared by the official planning bodies (Hudson, 1980).

It must be assumed that those who designed the system did not anticipate these problems of lack of coordination, increased centralisation, outdated zoning instruments and complex review procedures. What is surprising, however, is the slow response to initiate change to address those and other problems in the system. The net result is that spatial planning is viewed as being negative and not relevant to the current development agenda. In this chapter we examine land use changes, planned and unplanned, and the role and effectiveness of the planning system in promoting urban development and redevelopment.

Planning and Redevelopment

URBAN RENEWAL

Early Renewal Schemes

We saw in Chapter III that the problems of dilapidated and overcrowded housing conditions in Kingston were the primary concerns of the early planners in Jamaica. However, we also saw in Chapter III that despite this concern it was really the hurricane in 1951 that gave the main impetus to slum clearance and re-housing in the city. In 1951, the HHO took the opportunity to embark upon a slum clearance and re-housing scheme in Trench Town, which was extensively destroyed by the hurricane. By 1951, conditions in Kingston had deteriorated to such an extent that a total of 3,752 squatters were registered in four settlements in the West Kingston area (Clarke, 1975). The largest squatter settlements were Trench Town (2,613), Dung Hill (285), and Back-O-Wall (844). The settlement at Back-O-Wall had been in existence since 1935 and Trench Town dated back to the 1920s (Clarke, 1975).

The Tower Hill (Emergency Building Supplies Scheme) consisted of an area of seventy-two acres which was subdivided into 892 lots in a scheme to resettle squatters from Trench Town who had lost their homes during the hurricane. They were given a small grant for materials and charged a nominal amount for ground rent. There were originally no services other than roads. There was little development until 1964 when electricity, drains and water mains were installed, roads were resurfaced and the people were given the right to purchase the lots (Shankland/Cox, 1985). Although some initial clearance commenced after the hurricane it was not until 1968 that the government commissioned a study for the overall redevelopment of Trench Town. The proposed scheme covered an area of 246 acres and consisted of the development of 3,785 new dwellings together with new shopping areas, schools, libraries, clinics and public open spaces (Shankland/Cox, 1985). The first neighbourhood of 250 dwellings was completed in 1970. It consisted of three basic house types: single-storey, back-to-back houses planned in groups of four; two-storey houses; and two-storey units which were the single-storey units placed on top of each other instead of back to back (Shankland/Cox, 1985).

The Trench Town Redevelopment Scheme was followed by schemes in Tivoli Gardens (Back-O-Wall) (1971), McIntyre Lands (1978), and Denham Town (1989). These, together with some smaller schemes, accounted for 5,594 new units built between 1952 and 1989 in government slum clearance and re-housing schemes, with approximately 4,000 units constructed between 1952 and 1975 (McHardy, 1997b). By the 1970s, however, there was a change in policy as the government realised that its slum clearance and re-housing programme was not working for the following reasons: housing need was increasing as a result of the increasing population and slum clearance and re-housing were not addressing this need; the slum clearance schemes resulted in increasing housing need because of the demolition of many self-help buildings; and many of the re-housing schemes were beyond the affordability of the persons they were intended to benefit. The government also recognised that their policies were contributing to the housing problem rather providing solutions. Slum clearance and re-housing schemes were contributing to the deterioration of the housing opportunities of the poor, and were leading to an increase in squatter communities as the poor had to resort to peripheral locations in the city in order to meet their needs. In addition, the pursued policies came under increased criticism from housing experts and the international community such as the World Bank, USAID and other major lenders in the sector (McHardy, 1987d).

In 1972, the Ministry of Housing commissioned Shankland Cox Overseas to carry out a study of low-income needs in Kingston. The study entitled *Kingston Region Draft Low Income Strategy Report* analysed income structure in the city and recommended that sites and services be pursued as the option to house the poor. Based on this report the Ministry of Housing adopted the 'sites and services' concept as the basis of their housing policy. The sites and services programme which involved the provision of approximately 6,000 lots in four urban areas – KMA, Montego Bay, May Pen and Spanish Town – was funded by the World Bank. The programme also involved the upgrading of a number of squatter communities in an upgrading programme (McHardy, 1997d).

The sites and services concept has continued to be the main policy initiative for the provision of low-income housing since the 1970s, albeit with some modifications. In the 1980s the starter home programme replaced sites and services with the major modification being the provision of a subdivisible roofed 'core'. The programme for resettlement and integrated development enterprise ('Operation Pride') of the 1990s involves squatter upgrading and the distribution of serviced land to beneficiaries. The major differences between 'Operation Pride' and the other programmes are: 'Pride' projects are not necessarily specifically targeted at those below the median income; and communities must form themselves into cooperatives and set up community development funds to pay for the design of the scheme and infrastructure provision (McHardy, 1997d).

Kingston Waterfront Redevelopment

Although the poor housing conditions were considered one of the most serious redevelopment problems facing the country in the 1950s and 1960s, there was also at that time a growing recognition of the need to renew and expand the capital city and other towns. Kingston became the capital city for two major reasons. First, Kingston Harbour is one of the best natural harbours in the

menting a project of this nature (Knight, 1974). In 1966, a limited liability company, the Kingston Waterfront Development Company, was established under the chairmanship of the director of the corporation responsible for the creation of Newport West, pending the establishment of the Urban Development Corporation. At the same time, the government accepted an offer from the UK Ministry of Overseas Development to finance a plan for the area (Clarke, 1975). Steps were also taken to prepare and enact the Urban Development Corporation Law.

The Kingston Waterfront Development Company was established as a government-owned company charged with the responsibility to: acquire all the lands in the redevelopment area; ensure that a suitable plan was prepared for the development of these lands; implement or ensure the implementation of the plan; and do all these things within the framework of economic feasibility. The government, on the other hand would: hand over all lands owned by central government at a value to be agreed between the government and the company; lend the company sufficient funds to purchase land that was critical to the project; support the project in terms of providing any necessary infrastructure outside the area of the company's operation; and ensure that such assistance as was needed in terms of planning and building approvals pending promulgation of the UDC Act would be facilitated (Knight, 1974).

In 1968, Shankland Cox and Associates completed a plan for the area. They zoned the area for shops, offices, hotels, apartments, car parks, public open space and cultural activities. A hoverport to connect the city centre with the Norman Manley International airport at Palisadoes and a berth for cruise ships were also included. The plan also provided for a proposed road network linking the area with the general city network. In order to implement this plan one of the most important tasks facing the new company was land assembly. Ownership of land fell into four distinct groups, each having varying needs: the commercial port operators who had arranged to transfer part, but not all, of their operations to Newport West; the lumber importers and merchants who wished to expand their operations but could not be accommodated at Newport West; other private owners who were willing to move but wanted adequate compensation; and government properties (Knight, 1974).

It was recognised very early on that the normal procedures of acquiring land by private treaty and/or compulsory acquisition would not work because of the size and nature of the project. With regard to the commercial port operators it was agreed to purchase their land partly by means of land exchange, and partly by use of land bonds. Thus, some 1,674,000 square feet of land owned by the government at Newport West (obtained as royalty and tax from the development of the new port) was handed over to the wharf owners, Kingston Wharves. The lumber merchants were accommodated at Newport East, a former garbage dump on the foreshore which was acquired from the Jamaica Industrial Development Corporation by the Kingston Waterfront Development Company. The area was reclaimed and developed with deep water frontage. Government land was valued and treated as equity with the exception of one lot which required that the government departments and agencies be relocated before the land could be taken over. In addition, some of these departments needed port facilities but the site was required urgently. The company, therefore, provided land in Newport East in exchange for the lot and also constructed the office and pier facilities (with the government providing the funds) in order to facilitate the transfer in a timely manner (Knight, 1974).

Even before the plan for the project area was completed, plans for the promotion of land sales was underway. There were, however, differences of opinion regarding the disposal of land. The company's board and the planning consultants favoured leasehold arrangements for the land, but in view of the financial position of government it was decided that land would have to be sold. The sale of land commenced before the completion of the development plan for the area for the following reasons: there was a cash flow problem; it was felt that this would be a very lengthy process; and it was necessary to commence the project early (Knight, 1974). The Kingston Waterfront Development Company operated as the major developer for the Kingston Waterfront Project (Knight, 1974). Infrastructure work undertaken by the company included works undertaken on the government's behalf to ensure access to the area and that work which was an integral part of the project. The company proceeded on the basis of linking the timing of the project's infrastructure work to the sale of land. In this regard, design work was given out to consulting engineers as soon as they were prepared, but contracts to carry out work were awarded only when required by land sale and development (Knight, 1974). The first phase of the programme was completed in 1973 and the second phase in 1977. However, the economic crises of the late 1970s and early 1980s brought the project to a halt.

An effort to restart the redevelopment project was made in the mid-1980s with the opening of the Government Conference Centre in 1983. This centre was constructed as the headquarters of the International Seabed Authority. The Kingston Waterfront Company which had been dormant for some time was resurrected for the purpose of developing abandoned sites in and around the waterfront area. Although the International Seabed Authority has generated some activity, it has not been the catalyst for restarting the redevelopment process and its effects have been less than expected.

Impact of the Kingston Waterfront Redevelopment Project
The basic goal of the Kingston Waterfront Project was:

> to arrest and reverse the decline at the core, to make the area attractive again and to reconvert downtown into the focal point for shopping and entertainment on a regional basis.

(cited in George and Warren, 1984)

However, the project has not stimulated spontaneous renewal throughout the CBD as was anticipated. George and Warren (1984), in an evaluation of the waterfront project point out that there has not been a re-migration of commercial enterprises as approximately 65% of the commercial businesses are new. It would also appear from an analysis conducted by the UDC that most of the applicants for commercial space are non-CBD

105

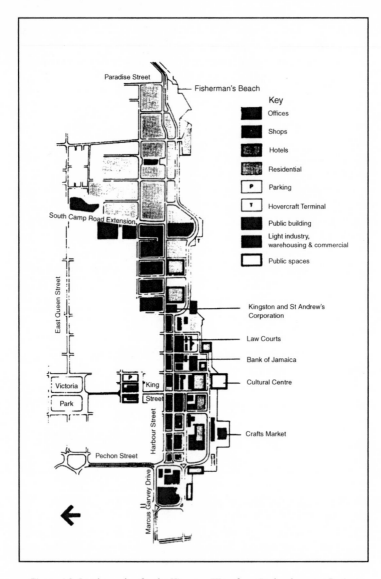

Figure 4.2: Land use plan for the Kingston Waterfront Redevelopment Project showing areas zoned for hotels, apartments and offices. However, not all the aims of this plan have been achieved.

businesses. Hill (1983), concluded:

> The majority of applicants received for the Kingston Mall and the Seabed Complex were for localized, i.e. non-central businesses. The applicants for retail establishments... are dominated by fast food restaurants that cater mainly to the local lunch-time traffic... In terms of non-food establishments, the applications were generally for small establishments with a mixture of functions, which do not seem capable of attracting customers throughout the Kingston region.

(cited in George and Warren, 1984)

Evidence that the project has not been successful in acting as a catalyst to promote further renewal in the city is very visible as the redeveloped area remains an enclave of new buildings surrounded by continuing blight and decay. In addition, some of the land uses proposed in the development plan were never implemented. For example, only one apartment complex and one of the two proposed hotels were constructed and that hotel is now used as offices by the Ministry of Health. The construction of apartments was designed to attract back to downtown Kingston some of the middle-class residents who were moving to the suburbs. George and Warren (1984) point out, however, that migration of middle-income residents has been small and the migrants are mainly professionals and not, as previously, the owners of businesses in the area. In fact, migration of middle-income residents to the area is related to the apartment complex only.

Several reasons have been put forward to the explain the failure of the Kingston Waterfront Project to stimulate development in the city core. Foremost among these is the development of uptown shopping and office areas. The growth of the suburban shopping plazas which have captured the upper- and middle-income clientele, leaving downtown Kingston as the main shopping area for the large low-income population which resides to the north-east of the waterfront. There are several reasons why the prime commercial areas of Kingston are located uptown. First, these areas are located in close proximity to where

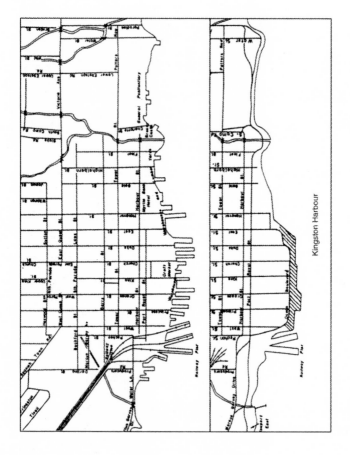

Figure 4.3: The old waterfront prior to redevelopment and the new waterfront after renewal.

people live, hence the distances to travel to work and shops are much shorter.

Second, the area is cleaner, buildings are modern and the surroundings generally more attractive. Third, there is no impetus to shop downtown which is viewed as poor. Thus, while construction costs are the same in suburban and downtown Kingston, the demand for rental space is much higher in uptown Kingston and rents are higher as a result. Another reason put forward for the failure of the waterfront project is the economic decline of the country since the late 1970s. The economic circumstances of the country have resulted in a number of enterprises going out of business and literally closing their doors. The abandoned buildings have fallen into disrepair and some buildings have been vandalised by those living nearby. Compounding this problem are a number of concerns which the business community in downtown Kingston feel must be addressed to enable the private sector to continue to strengthen its economic base. The three major concerns are security, sanitation and sewage disposal in the downtown area. Security concerns relate to the need to change the perception of both Jamaicans and visitors that downtown Kingston is a dangerous place to travel and shop. With regard to sanitation there is a need for better street cleaning and upgraded solid waste collection and removal from residential and commercial buildings in the downtown area. Even with the recent reconstruction of sewerage there are still concerns about long-term sewage collection and treatment downtown (Grossman et al, 1994).

In addition to these major concerns, the business community downtown also feels that there are other issues which complicate the issue of transformation of the area and the return of its shopping importance. There is continued conflict between the informal vendor-community operating downtown and store operators. Although off-street market areas have been set aside for these vendors many operate on the sidewalks leading to complaints by store owners that their businesses are affected as a result. In addition, the off-street market areas are in an unsatisfactory state and the refurbishing of the market area to the northwest of the waterfront is in an incomplete state. The presence of a low-income residential community in close proximity to the downtown commercial area is viewed also as a major problem for regeneration of the area by the business community (Grossman et al, 1994).

RENEWAL PROJECTS OF THE 1990s

Kingston Restoration Company

The setting up of the Kingston Restoration Company Limited (KRC) was another major initiative in the re-generation of downtown Kingston. In 1983, a group of leading businesses and the Urban Development Corporation came together to form the KRC. The mission of the company is to halt the decay and restore downtown Kingston for economic activity and employment opportunities. In order to achieve this goal, the inner Kingston Development Project was launched by the KRC in 1986. It targeted an area of a hundred blocks which included the major commercial district and residential communities. Supported by the government of Jamaica and USAID, the project was implemented between 1986 and 1996.

The aims of the project were to demonstrate that derelict buildings could be rehabilitated and put to productive use, and to help restore inner Kingston as a centre for economic activity and job creation. These objectives were achieved through the implementation of four programmes: the development of industrial and commercial properties; the provision of restoration or small grants for building improvements; improvements to streets and public places; and community development.

By 1996, the KRC had created 15,421.7 square metres of factory space compared to a target of 30,146.05 square metres, and 6,165 square metres of the 6,642.35 square metres targeted for commercial space. In addition, 6,234 jobs were created almost doubling the target of 3,500 jobs under this programme. The restoration grants programme facilitates business expansion by small downtown businesses through the provision of grants of up to 20% of the cost of restoration amounting to as much as a maximum of US $3,000. The programme has accounted for 22,954.93 square metres of retail space as a result of approximately forty-three grants. The KRC has also undertaken the improvement of King and Duke Streets, two of the city's main thoroughfares. Street improvement, facade improvement and the reconstruction of sidewalks have significantly enhanced these two corridors.

An integral component of the KRC Inner Kingston Development Project was community development as there was growing recognition in the 1980s that urban renewal involved more than the restoration of buildings. Consequently, significant investment has been made into human development through several social programmes. The Youth Educational Support System (YESS) was introduced to address the problem of a high drop-out rate among high school students in the community. Teenagers, and young adults are the focus of this leadership development programme. Scholarship assistance, supervised homework sessions and tuition are some of the programmes instituted by the KRC. Three hundred and fourteen participants are served annually by YESS. In addition to academic support, YESS students are involved in other activities designed to enhance their social development and leadership ability. In addition, the YESS students are responsible for the maintenance of the Teen Centre which is the home base of their activities. The Teen Centre is part of a larger complex managed by the KRC which also houses a library, a health clinic and photographic lab. The KRC is also helping to address security and crime prevention needs in the community through collaboration with the police in implementing community policing initiatives. The KRC acquired and restored the police station and employed staff to liase between the community and the police.

With the Inner Kingston Development Project coming to a close, the KRC contracted the physical planning division of the University of Technology (UTech) and a team of professionals in 1994 to undertake the preparation of a plan for the development of Jones Town, one of Kingston's inner city communities.

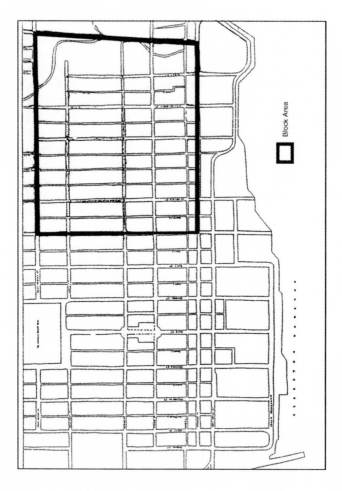

Block Area

Figure 4.9: Area targeted by KRC for restoration. Known as the inner Kingston development project it promoted the restoration of industrial and commercial properties in an area covering one hundred blocks.

The KRC then approached the British Government in 1994 for technical and financial assistance, and in 1997 the British Government and the Government of Jamaica signed the Jamaica Urban Poverty Project Memorandum (UPP). The goal of the UPP is to contribute to the improvement of the quality of life in poor urban communities in Kingston, starting in Jones Town. It envisages that the lessons learned in Jones Town will be replicated in communities faced with similar problems. The UPP will also enhance the capacity of the KRC to lead the process of replicating the community-led participation process in urban areas.

Although the KRC has achieved considerable success in its performance to date, the extent to which it has been able to stimulate the redevelopment process has been limited. There are many reasons for this. First, the project investments made by the KRC have been funded mainly by grant funds from USAID in the past and currently from the British Government. Second, because funding has been principally from grant sources the level of funding has not been large. Moderate levels of grant funds limit the size and scope of the projects undertaken by the KRC. Third, while the KRC has completed the refurbishing of four major buildings and provided approximately forty-three restoration grants it has not been able to maintain a sustained programme of private sector renewal activities. The KRC was not able to ensure that the private sector would be spurred into action and continue rehabilitating dilapidated buildings once USAID funds ceased. Related to this is the supply of properties available to the KRC and the supply of those suitable for conversion to industrial use was soon exhausted. Finally, the KRC does not have the organisational capacity to undertake a large urban renewal programme involving complex land re-assembly and financing.

As was the case with the Kingston Waterfront Project, the KRC has been forced to operate outside of the planning system as the Kingston Development Order offered little assistance. The KRC, like the Kingston Waterfront Development Company, had to seek help in the preparation of a plan to undertake development work on the urban poverty project. This problem of the absence of a plan to guide development activities in the city led the KRC to commission the preparation of a master plan for the redevelopment of downtown Kingston, called Vision 20/20. With financial and technical assistance from USAID, the KRC set out to create a plan for the economic and social development of the historic core of the capital city. The study area was defined as the Downtown Kingston Development Area (DKDA). The DKDA is an area of approximately three hundred square blocks that extends from the waterfront.

In order to ensure that there would be a common vision for the DKDA and ownership of the plan by all relevant agencies, the KRC created a public and private sector partnership to oversee plan preparation. In 1992, the KRC set up a committee with members coming from the UDC, Town Planning Department, Town and Country Planning Authority, KSAC and the Jamaica Chamber of Commerce (JCC). Administered by the KRC, the committee was charged with the responsibility of preparing a plan which analysed the issues of a decaying downtown Kingston and hoped to reverse the social and economic consequences. The plan was prepared through a series of fifty-three community discussions and presentations, including eleven public forums. Completed in 1994, Vision 20/20 is still to be implemented. The plan has not been implemented partly because of the economic downturn in the country, and partly because there is no single institution charged with its implementation. Only the Urban Development Corporation has the organisational structure and capacity to undertake a project of this nature and it is anticipated that once the economic circumstances have improved the UDC will proceed with the implementation of Vision 20/20.

The Tax Incentive Programme

In an effort to get private sector capital committed to urban renewal in a more sustained manner, the government, in 1995, passed into law the Urban Renewal (Tax Relief) Act, and introduced the tax incentive programme for urban renewal (TIP). The rationale behind the programme is rooted in the desire to motivate the private sector to assume the major role for redevelopment of blighted areas in downtown Kingston. The purpose of the programme is to offer incentives to the private developer so that he may recoup his investments and thus be willing to put capital in what would be considered, under normal circumstances, an unwise investment. Through the TIP, the government will offer tax relief as an incentive to individuals or companies which undertake capital investment in blighted areas, starting in Kingston. The minister responsible for urban development in consultation with the local authorities and the Town and Country Planning Authority, will define and identify those areas which will benefit under the programme. Downtown Kingston is the first area to benefit from the TIP followed by Port Royal Special Development Area and more recently the Montego Bay Special Development Area.

The Urban Development Corporation (UDC), acting as agents of the Ministry of Finance, will act as a clearing house for all applications under the programme. A Programme Executing Unit (PEU), has been established within the UDC. The PEU incorporates an Incentive Recommendations Committee (IRC), which will have both public and private sector representation. The IRC will ensure that applications meet the requirements and intent of the law and make recommendations to the Ministry of Finance. To be considered for incentives one must apply for either 'approved developer' or 'approved organisation' status. To apply for either status the relevant application form must be submitted along with the relevant documents and application fee to the PEU.

There are three categories of incentive: urban renewal bonds; investment tax credit and tax relief on rental income. Urban renewal bonds may be issued or underwritten by approved private and public sector organisations for the sole purpose of mobilising funds for specific projects within blighted areas. Bonds will provide benefits to three distinct groups: issuers, investors and user of funds from the bonds. Approved organisations from both private and public sectors will issue or underwrite bonds (issuers) and will be eligible for tax free interest during the incentive period if the proceeds are loaned to approved developers and investment tax credit on funds used by the issuers who carry out their own development. Individuals or corporate investors in bonds will enjoy tax free interest on these bonds. Approved developers who undertake projects which are financed from bond proceeds will enjoy investment tax credit on the funds used for the development and tax free rental income from the developed property within the incentive period. In addition to income tax relief, the urban renewal bonds will be exempt from transfer tax and stamp duty.

The government will provide incentives for either the construction of new buildings or improvement of old ones. This will be available to approved developers, in the form of investment tax credit of 25% on capital sums invested, set off against other income tax liability of the developer, from any other source, but limited to 50% of that liability in any one year of assessment. Developers must prove 'approved developer' status to the income tax department at the time of filing tax returns. Tax free rental income will be available to approved developers in the form of full relief from income tax on rental income from the new refurbished buildings, during the incentive period.

It is still too early to determine the success of the TIP. Since its commissioning in 1995 and up to November 1999, close to J $1 billion has been invested in projects downtown under the TIP. Concerns raised include charging an application fee which some feel will be a disincentive to investors; while others feel that there is a need for a development plan to ensure that investments that take place in these areas are desirable.

Planned Urban Expansion

PLANNED OFFICE DEVELOPMENT

New Kingston

As indicated earlier one of the major factors which triggered the waterfront redevelopment project was the decline in economic activity of the downtown area brought about by the emergence of rival business districts in response to the growing suburban population. The concentration of office buildings in New

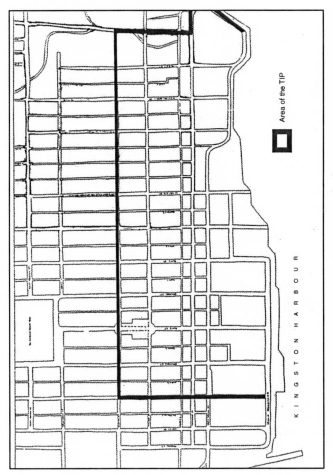

Figure 4.11: The first area to benefit under the TIP includes a section of downtown Kingston which focuses on the old historic core. The TIP is expected to play a catalytic role in arresting decay and rejuvenating this area.

KINGSTON HARBOUR

Area of the TIP

Kingston poses the greatest threat to the regeneration of down-town Kingston as New Kingston today is the main centre for the important offices and hotels located in the city. While the Kingston waterfront and New Kingston are competing for the same clientele, both were very large projects which required some form of public-private partnership in order to facilitate their implementation. However, the nature of these partnerships varied considerably. In the case of the Kingston waterfront redevelopment project a more planning-led approach was taken. Knight (1975) refers to the importance of this partnership in the waterfront redevelopment project in the following statement:

> ...there seemed to be no suitable institution which could implement a plan of such major proportions, which clearly needed the powers of Government, as well as the elasticity and dynamism of private enterprise.

> (Knight, 1974)

The absence of a suitable institution led the government, through the then ministry with portfolio responsibility, the Ministry of Development and Welfare, to initiate a study of the New Towns Act of the United Kingdom. The New Towns Act was the model on which the Urban Development Corporation Act was based and also the institutional framework for the implementation of the Kingston Waterfront Redevelopment Project (Knight, 1974).

The promulgation of the UDC Act and the establishment of the Urban Development Corporation indicates the importance of the plan-led approach in the waterfront project. As set out in Chapter III, under its Act, the UDC must prepare a development plan for its designated areas. Although the Kingston Waterfront Redevelopment Company was established pending promulgation of the UDC Act, the British Government provided financial and technical support for the preparation of a development plan for the area. Shankland Cox and Associates were appointed in November 1966 to prepare a plan in two years and submitted their final version together with a model of the proposed project in December 1968. Private sector participation in the process was reflected in the composition of the board of the redevelopment company, with a number of board members being drawn from the private sector.

While the 1946 New Towns Act provided the model for the establishment of the UDC there are some important differences between the New Towns Act and the UDC Act. The New Towns Act gave power to the minister responsible for planning to formally designate new towns. A Ministry of Town and Country Planning had been set up in 1943 and this was one of its first important functions (Hall, 1992). The minister would then set up a development corporation responsible for the construction and management of the town. In sharp contrast to Britain, in Jamaica the Urban Development Corporation is set up as both a planning organisation and a developer, which has led to a host of problems as was discussed in Chapter III. Foremost among these is the complete separation of the activities of the UDC from the purview of town and country planning. Of great concern also is the lack of involvement of the local authorities in activities undertaken by the UDC in their parishes.

While the Kingston waterfront redevelopment was plan-led, the New Kingston project was developer-led. New Kingston is developed on 32.38 hectares of land which was the former Knutsford Park, Jamaica's primary race track for sixty years before its closing in 1959 (Ransom, 1985). The original idea for the subdivision of this site came from Keble Jobson, a land surveyor responsible for many developments in St Andrew. He approached the then chairman of Knutsford Park Limited who supported the idea of subdividing the area and after reviewing a preliminary plan bought out the other shareholders (Ransom, 1985). Around 1957, the land parcel was sold to New Kingston Suburban Developments Limited, a consortium of entrepreneurs who put up the money to purchase the land and who were to be the administering body for the subdivision. This body was to form a loose structure, meeting annually to discuss matters related to the subdivision.

By mid-1977, press releases appeared heralding the sale of the race track and its transformation into a modern township. Reports emphasised that the new development would be more than a traditional subdivision, as it would be designed along city planning principles. The development was to include typical CBD commercial and office uses, such as banks, department stores, hotels, restaurants etc. The area was called New Kingston for the precise reason that it was to become the new commercial and office centre in the capital city. New Kingston was seen as the solution to the congestion and traffic problems downtown, and the growing dereliction of the area. The new development would eliminate most of the deterrents to locating downtown by providing improved access with wide boulevards, improved parking, and a well-designed interior street system.

The plan called for the subdivision of 1.1 million square feet into 358 small lots with an average of 3,000 square feet. The majority of the lots of the development were laid out in 30' x 90' rectangular shape. Sale of lots by square foot was not the usual method of the time but rather by total lot price. Developers were expected to group lots to make larger sites for more extensive projects. Because the TPD had no standards for lot sizes at the time the market primarily determined lot sizes (Ransom, 1985). The small lot sizes selected for New Kingston in some way shaped the direction of the subdivision that would develop. In this regard, the larger and less expensive lots in other development projects attracted the suburban shopping plazas and supermarkets as they had more available parking. New Kingston on the other hand was more suited to office development (Ransom, 1985).

Initial development of the subdivision was speculative. The demand for lots which was active at the start tapered off in the 1960s and lots which were sold were not built on for several years. All the lots along the main thoroughfare were only J $2.50 per square foot when they were first placed on the market. By 1972, lots averaged J $25.00 to J $30.00 per square foot and J $60.00 to J $80.00 per square foot in 1985 (Ransom, 1985). The first major building to be constructed was the Sheraton Wyndham Hotel in 1962. Between 1962 and 1969, four buildings were constructed and nine more were constructed between 1971 and 1979. There was very little construction activity between 1979 and 1984, when the insurance company, Life of Jamaica, embarked on its massive development programme.

In 1969, the Town Planning Department and the KSAC evaluated

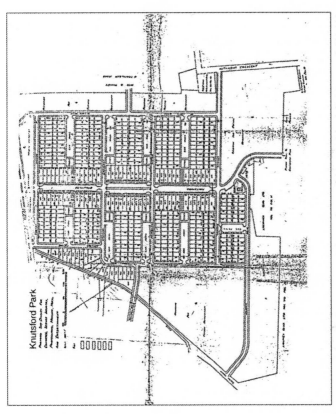

Figure 4.12: The original subdivision plan of New Kingston. The total area of the original subdivision was 2,301,000 square feet, of which 1.1 million square feet were divided into 358 lots and seven blocks were not subdivided but reserved for future use.

parking in New Kingston. The concern was the application of the parking ratio requirements established in the 1966 Kingston Development Order and their impact on small and large building developments within the subdivision. As a result, service roads were instituted between adjoining lots to reduce problems of loading in the front of buildings and to give better parking solutions to buildings so that staff parking would take place in the back lots while short-term parking would be reserved for the front of the buildings (Ransom, 1985).

At the time at which the roads were designed there was no idea that the traffic would reach the volumes found in the area today. When the roads were first laid out traffic planning was a relatively new concept in Jamaica. For example, in 1964, a comprehensive analysis of traffic flows in the KMA undertaken by the British Road Institute indicated that estimates appeared unreliable and annual growth rates were low as they were based solely on downtown Kingston. Increases in Kingston were expected to be small due to congestion and limitations imposed by the capacity of those roads (Ransom, 1985). In 1990, the traffic problem in New Kingston was extremely problematic as acceptable capacities had been exceeded despite several traffic management initiatives to deal with the problem.

The developer-led New Kingston development is evident in some of the criticism raised about the project. One of the most strident criticisms is the lack of planning associated with the development. Although there were zoning proposals, there is no evidence of an overall objective and strategy on the part of the promoters (Ransom, 1985). There was no overall development plan linked to investment criteria and decision making as was the case in the Kingston Waterfront Redevelopment Project. The lack of an overall plan was one of the main reasons for the change in the direction of growth and development from that which was originally conceived. For example, the absence of recreational and residential uses in the area was not in the original plan which was to have been a mixture of commercial, residential and offices. The original plan also envisaged the development of green spaces, but this aspect of the development was never followed through by Suburban Developments Limited.

PLANNED TOURISM DEVELOPMENTS

When the UDC was established in 1968, it was given the authority to acquire, hold and dispose of land and to plan for and undertake development in its designated areas. The UDC carries out this mandate by: designating a selected area for development, wherein the corporation will have full powers under the law; acquiring lands within the designated area and formulating a development plan; and constructing primary infrastructure and promoting secondary development. While the UDC had primary responsibility for the redevelopment of the Kingston waterfront it is also the entity which has been at the forefront of the development of other towns in Jamaica. The north coast town of Ocho Rios and sections of Negril and Montego Bay have been intensively developed by the UDC to promote tourism, including the building of several large hotels.

Montego Bay Waterfront Development

Situated north on the mouth of the Montego River, the town built its reputation as a tourist centre around Doctor's Cave Beach, a white sand beach in the immediate area. UDC's involvement began in 1970 with a study of the area, followed by the launching of the Montego Bay Development Company. The UDC prepared a project for the development of Montego Bay with the initial primary development involving the reclamation of lands, making of public beaches and the construction of a link road.

The Caribbean Development Bank approved a loan to assist in the financing of the project. The loan was granted for the construction and improvement of 3,883 feet of highway, construction of bridges, the extension of sewerage facilities and the improvement of drainage to be undertaken by the UDC. The project included: the reclamation of 21.9 hectares of land; redevelopment of 4.5 hectares of existing land; improvement of drainage; improvement of the city's road network including the construction of a completely new stretch of road on the reclaimed land; a small extension of the sewerage disposal system; construction and protection of about 1.4 hectares of public beach; and provision of approximately 18.6 hectares of saleable land.

The project included a secondary phase of development inde-

123

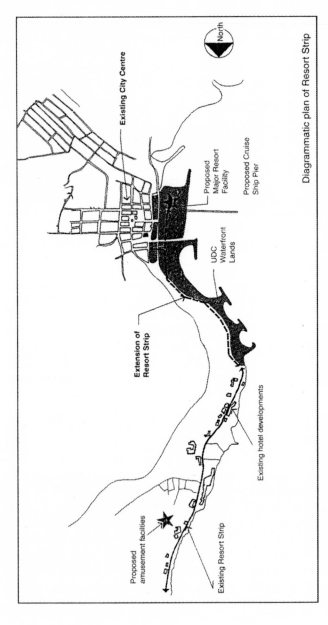

Figure 4.15: In the 1970s the UDC initiated a waterfront project to enhance the visitor's experience in the central area of Montego Bay.

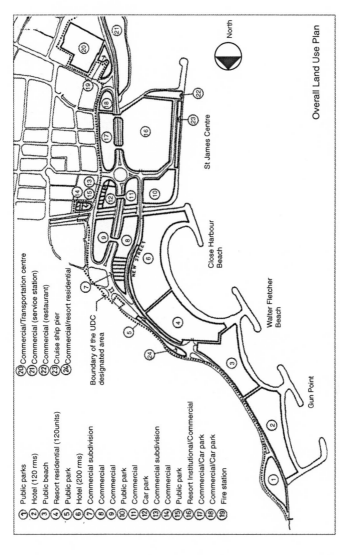

① Public parks
② Hotel (120 rms)
③ Public beach
④ Resort residential (120units)
⑤ Public park
⑥ Hotel (200 rms)
⑦ Commercial subdivision
⑧ Commercial
⑨ Commercial
⑩ Public park
⑪ Commercial
⑫ Car park
⑬ Commercial subdivision
⑭ Commercial
⑮ Public park
⑯ Resort Institutional/Commercial
⑰ Commercial/Car park
⑱ Commercial/Car park
⑲ Fire station
⑳ Commercial/Transportation centre
㉑ Commercial (service station)
㉒ Commercial (restaurant)
㉓ Cruise ship pier
㉔ Commercial/resort residential

Boundary of the UDC designated area

North

Overall Land Use Plan

St James Centre

Close Harbour Beach

Walter Fletcher Beach

Gun Point

NEW STREET

Figure 4.16: Original plan for proposed land uses in the UDC waterfront project for Montego Bay. Uses proposed included those designed to expand the tourism product and improve local civic facilities.

pendent of the primary phase. Included in the secondary phase are the construction of facilities for the expansion of tourism and commerce, as well as local civic activities.

Ocho Rios

The development of Ocho Rios as a major resort and commercial centre was a major undertaking of the UDC with the establishment of the St Ann's Bay Development Company in 1969. At this time much of the town's development was in the east and west with the central area being pockets of squatter settlements. The UDC, through the St Ann's Bay Development Company, acquired substantial land holdings and set about transforming the area. These activities included land reclamation and beach creation, upgrading of roads, construction of sidewalks and drainage channels, provision of sewerage and electricity, and secondary development including hotels, commercial buildings and residential development.

The rapid transformation of Ocho Rios from a fishing village into a major resort has resulted in inadequate development of social and physical infrastructure. Due to the primacy of tourism in Ocho Rios, a relatively large number of persons migrate to the area in search of tourism related jobs. This process is exerting pressure on the housing market in and around the town, exceeding the capacity of the formal market to cope with the situation. As a result, informal housing has been growing rapidly in and around the town of Ocho Rios. This has created problems for Ocho Rios both in terms of orderly residential development and the potential negative impact on the environment and the tourist industry. Between 1970 and 1988, there were three informal settlements in and around the town of Ocho Rios, namely Green Bay, Steer Town and Buckfield. Since 1988 other settlements have appeared in Belmont, Roaring River and Mammee Bay. The government has undertaken projects to resettle these squatters (Roaring River 1 and 2, and Mansfield), but new squatters often take the place of those who have been relocated.

A plan for the development of the town of Ocho Rios and its outlying areas was completed by the Town Planning Department in 1994 and a Provisional Development Order for the Parish of St Ann was promulgated in 1998 and confirmed in 1999. This development order is the first order which has been prepared in some detail drawing heavily from the development plan. The order sets out a strategy which establishes the main direction in which the future development and use of land in the parish are to take place and reflects the general features which are necessary to secure a proper balance between the competing demands for land. The development strategy for St Ann is to promote a balanced and multi-centred development pattern over a ten year period with respect to the available physical and social infrastructure and to the protection of the built and natural environment.

Negril

In 1968 and 1969 the UDC purchased large private tracts of land (approximately 809 hectares), in the Negril Green Island Development Order area and designated land under the 1968 UDC Act with a view to coordinating and implementing a comprehensive development programme for the area. In 1969, a master plan was produced by Adelatec for the UDC lands. In 1971, Betchel produced a detailed master plan for 39.3 hectares, and the UDC proceeded with the implementation of stages 1, 2 and 3 of Betchel proposals. In 1968 and 1971, legislation was introduced to encourage resort development; the Hotel Incentives Act and the Resort Cottage Incentive Act, respectively. In 1982, Design Collaborative prepared a development plan for the UDC's designated lands and in 1984 the Negril Green Island Confirmed Development Order was promulgated. These actions were undertaken in order to develop the eleven mile strip of white sand beaches into a prime tourist location.

Negril has become the island's third most important resort centre and its fine white sand beach has attracted a large number of hotels around Long Bay and Rutland Point. However, planning and management of the area is thwart with problems and as a consequence, enforcement and compliance with laws and regulations have not met the required standards making it difficult to mobilise investors and financial resources for development. The crux of the problem lies in the complex mechanisms for planning and development in Negril. There are several institutions which operate in the area and which affect planning and development, namely, the Negril Green Island Planning

Authority, the TCPA, the UDC, the Westmoreland Parish Council and the Hanover Parish Council. In addition, Negril has, during different periods of its history, been under the control of different institutions.

As we saw in Chapter III, Section 11(1) of the Town and Country Planning Act allows the minister to set up a special local planning authority in respect of any area situated in two or more parishes. With this in mind the Negril Area Land Authority (NALA) was appointed by the Minister of Agriculture (minister responsible for planning) in 1959 as the local planning authority with responsibility for development control in the 1959 Confirmed Development Order. In the mid-1970s, however, the TCPA 'called in' development control applications under Section 12 of the Town and Country Planning Act.

In 1981, the TCPA published a new provisional development order and in that same year, the government decided to phase out the NALA. The reasons given for this were that the authority had not operated as a land authority, but rather as a local planning authority with planning powers under the Town and Country Planning Act and further that, for several years the authority had not had these powers under the Act since the area was 'called in'. With the phasing out of the NALA, its assets were taken over by the UDC and planning powers under the new provisional development order were vested in the UDC's subsidiary company for Negril. This company therefore became the local planning authority with planning powers under the Town and Country Planning Act. All government land in the area not owned by the UDC which was being used, or for which there was no proposed use, was vested in the UDC. A number of problems arose from these decisions. Foremost among them was that the UDC's subsidiary company would now become both the developer and the local planning authority, vested with the power to receive development applications, deal with them, issue enforcement notices and see generally to the orderly and progressive development of the order area.

From February 1981 until 15 May 1981 there was an absence of a body to take over the powers and duties performed by the NALA. Consequently, the minister responsible for planning appointed the GTP as the local planning authority for the area. Enforcement, however, was a problem so after discussion on the matter it was decided that the relevant parish councils (Westmoreland and Hanover) would undertake these functions. However, there were no funds allocated to this exercise upon closure of the NALA. Severe financial constraints and limited capacity of the parish councils meant development control activities were severely curtailed. There was a rapid and undesirable deterioration of the area. Illegal developments, non-conforming uses, and ad hoc and uncontrolled development took place making accessibility difficult along the rocky coastline and cliff edge.

Based on the deteriorating conditions in Negril it was decided that a new development order should be prepared and that the area under development control be expanded in the new order, bringing Negril Village under its purview. A provisional development order was published in 1981 with an expanded development order area. It was also recognised that there was a need for a local planning authority to be sited in the Negril Development Order Area in order to carry out the planning functions under the Town and Country Planning Act.

In March 1984, the Negril Green Island Area Local Planning Authority (NGIALPA) was established and the provisional development order was confirmed. However, the local planning authority is not an autonomous body as Negril is 'called in'. All development applications must be forwarded to the TCPA for planning approval and to the respective parish council for building approvals. Development control is also not working in Negril because of the division of responsibility for development planning and environmental planning among several agencies renders coordination difficult and often causes long delays in the approval process. In addition, severe financial constraints and the limited capacity of the local planning authority make it difficult for the organisation to carry out its functions. Another issue of concern is the sensitive environment of Negril. It is important therefore that all development activities in the area conform with the development order, particularly with regard to densities.

Urban Growth and Decentralisation

PLANNED DECENTRALISATION

The Background

In terms of urban and rural distribution, indications are that the country has become increasingly urban since 1960 when only 34% of the population lived in towns and cities compared to 50.2% in 1991. Between 1970 and 1990 the urban population has increased overall by 14% at a rate of 2.1% per annum compared to an overall increase of only 2% for the rural population (Statistical Institute of Jamaica, 1995). The result is that by 1991 the population was equally divided between these areas.

In 1970, the largest city, the Kingston Metropolitan Area (KMA) had a population of 475,548 and was approximately eleven times the size of the next largest town, Montego Bay. This skewed development of the urban system has emerged for historical reasons. The development of the Jamaican economy proceeded from port towns which linked a raw material producing hinterland with external markets in developed countries. In the interior, numerous small towns and larger villages grew to serve as trading and distributing centres for the surrounding countryside and remain important market towns.

The over concentration of economic activities in these centres set in motion a pattern of urbanisation which tends to enhance their dominance. This is particularly true of the KMA. By 1943, the KMA contained 80.8% of the urban population and although it has remained the chief target for rural-urban migration, between 1943 and 1960 there was a further widening of this gap. Economies accruing through the existence of transport facilities, public utilities, availability of skilled labour, and technical, financial and managerial services led to the continued attraction of the capital city as the location for new economic activities, particularly manufacturing industries. The polarisation of urban development in the KMA and the relative stagnation of the rural parishes resulted in the city becoming the chief magnet for migrants from the countryside between 1943 and 1960. Since the 1960s, however, there have been changes in the rate and pattern of urban growth.

While most of the population growth experienced by the capital city in the decade of 1960 to 1970 took place within the boundaries of the Kingston Metropolitan Area, the surrounding urban townships of Yallahs, Spanish Town, May Pen and Old Harbour were also affected. While in the previous decade the problems of each urban centre was small enough to have been dealt with on a local basis, by 1970 it was recognised that suburbanisation was spilling over into the adjoining parishes of St Catherine, Clarendon and St Thomas and urban growth could no longer be addressed on an individual township basis.

Consequently, the United Nations Development Programme project 'Assistance in Physical Development Planning' which had just completed a National Physical Plan for Jamaica from 1970 to 1990 was asked to prepare a plan for the Kingston region. The National Physical Plan and the process involved in its preparation will be discussed in Chapter V. In 1973, the *Kingston Regional Plan* was published in response to the need for overall planning for an area which stretched from Clarendon Park in the west to the Salt Ponds in the east. The feeling at that time was that transportation systems, public utilities, land use etc., in the defined area were regional issues which demanded a regional approach to their solution. The plan approached the problems of the area with four main needs in view, namely more effective control of urban development; the planning and development of new towns and extensions of existing urban areas in the region; the reservation of land for agriculture, conservation and recreation; and coordination of the decisions of various government and private agencies within the region. The major goals of the *Kingston Regional Plan* are outlined below:

> The continued growth and development of the Kingston Region promises its citizens a higher standard of living. However, attempts must be made to bring a sense of order and purpose to physical development as it takes place. If this is not done the net result of development will be a deteriorating quality of life for the citizens. The Regional Plan therefore is a first step towards bringing order and purpose to the development of the Kingston Region.

> (Kingston Regional Plan, 1973)

The plan estimated that new urban land would have to be developed in order to accommodate an additional 175,000 urban dwellers. Based on an urban density of sixteen persons per acre the plan estimated that this would require a minimum of eighteen, to a maximum of thirty-five square miles of new land. A survey to determine the location and extent of land physically suitable for new urban development in the region ended with land being allocated into one of three categories as set out in Table II.

Table II: *Land Physically Suitable for New Urban Development*

Category	Potential	Characteristics	Example
I	Suitable for urban development	Dominance of low and relatively low constraints	Hellshire; various areas north of Spanish Town and May Pen Highway
II	Further investigation required	Constraints not highly dominant	Balance of land between Spanish Town and May Pen not in Category I
III	Least suitable for urban development Unsuitable for urban development	Dominance of a high degree of constraints	Fertile plains of St Catherine and Clarendon Slopes of Port Royal Mountains Coastal swamps

Source: *Kingston Regional Plan*, p.13

The plan determined that within Category I there were seventy-five square miles which were physically suitable for additional urban development. The development of this land would make no inroads on land of good agricultural capability, would avoid steep slopes and would be comparatively well drained. Based on the location and extent of land designated as being in Category I for new urban development the plan designed four alternatives for the form urban structure should take for the region by 1990. The four alternatives for future urban structure outlined in the plan are set out in Table III.

Table III: *Alternative Forms of Future Urban Structure*

Category	Development Concept	Urban Centres Involved
A	New urban development as close as possible to Kingston. Main emphasis on the development of Hellshire Hills.	St Thomas Coast, Kingston, Portmore/Braeton, Hellshire Hills, Spanish Town, Old Harbour, May Pen
B	New urban development as close as possible to Kingston. Main emphasis on a new urban belt extending from Spanish Town to Old Harbour north of the main road	As above, with only minor development in Hellshire and main emphasis on a 'new town' belt extending from Spanish Town to Old Harbour
C	New urban development as close as possible to Kingston with a parallel and balanced development of Hellshire Hills and the proposed 'new town' belt city	As above but with equal emphasis on Hellshire and 'new town'
D	Dispersed urban development balanced between six centres external to Kingston	Kingston, St Thomas Coast, Portmore/Braeton, Hellshire, Spanish Town, Old Harbour and May Pen

Source: *Kingston Regional Plan*, p.13 and p.14

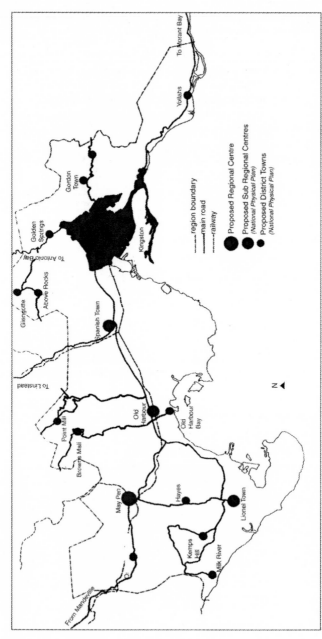

Figure 4.18: *The Kingston Regional Plan*, 1973 defined the region as extending from Clarendon Park in the west to the Salt Ponds in St Thomas in the east. The region is dominated by the KMA; the other major urban centres are Spanish Town, Old Harbour and May Pen.

Further examination and investigation of these four alternatives led to the further study of alternatives A and B. The basic difference between these two alternatives was whether the emphasis on the development of new urban land should be Hellshire Hills (A) or in the proposed urban belt between Spanish Town and Old Harbour (B). The economic evaluation (cost-benefit analysis) of the two selected alternatives was carried out in two phases. The first phase looked at costs of infrastructure and public services over the twenty-five year period, while the second dealt with the estimated costs and benefits of both public and private investment. The conclusions of the economic analyses were: the overall benefit:cost ratio of the two alternatives were identical so that whichever alternative was selected nothing would be lost in terms of economic efficiency; alternative A would require a higher capital investment than alternative B but would yield significantly higher returns; as capital investment would be made over a twenty year period alternative A was considered preferable in order to benefit from the higher returns. Alternative A was selected by the then government as the strategy for future urban development in the Kingston region. The plan indicated that major implications of the population distribution which would result from following the recommended urban strategy from alternative A would be as shown in Table IV.

Indications that the 1973 *Kingston Regional Plan* has gone awry are reflected in the population figures from the 1991 population census. While the region experienced rapid change in terms of population size and land use, this was not quite in the manner of the recommended urban strategy. Based on the 1991 census Portmore's population was 93,799 on census day. By 1995 it was estimated that the population of Portmore had grown to 174,000. Hellshire's population on the other hand was estimated to be approximately 2,400 in 1995. One of the reasons for the proposed strategy not achieving its stated objectives is reflected in the rate and pattern of urban growth in Jamaica.

Table IV: *Major Urban Centres*

Urban centre	Population 1970	Projected 1990	Mode of Increase
Kingston	506,000	590,000	Infill within existing metropolitan area boundary
Portmore-Braeton	5,000	100,000	Infill plus planning and development to accommodate an additional 35,000 persons over and above land presently committed to residential development
Hellshire		120,000	Continuation of present planning to meet target population of 120,000
Spanish Town	42,000	150,000	Infill of existing urban areas plus 50,000
Old Harbour-Old Harbour Bay	10,000	50,000	Infill and expansion of existing urban areas by a total of 40,000
May Pen	26,000	50,000	Infill within the existing urban area of 24,000
Infill in existing subdivisions Yallahs to Old Harbour		40,000	Infill in existing subdivisions by 40,000
TOTAL	589,000	1,100,000	Population increment 511,000

Source: *Kingston Regional Plan*, p.15

With regard to the rate of urban growth, for the majority of parishes the rate of urbanisation was greatest between 1960 and 1970. Data from the population censuses indicate that during the period of 1960 to 1970 the rate of urban growth was 3%. However, this declined to 2.2% between 1970 and 1982 and 1.2% between 1982 and 1991. Despite this decline, the rate of urbanisation proceeded at a higher rate than overall population growth during the corresponding periods (1.39%, 1.42%, 0.86% respectively). The slow down of urban growth since 1970 has meant that population increment in the Kingston region was less than projected in Table IV. The actual increase between 1970 and 1990 was approximately 217,000 compared with a projected increment of 471,000 (excluding infill of subdivisions between Yallahs and Old Harbour).

As indicated in Chapter II there are indications that Kingston's dominance as a primary city is slipping somewhat. In terms of percentage share of the total urban population, the KMA remains the chief urban centre with 55.9% of the urban population in 1991 (including Portmore), but declining from 72% in 1960 to 67% in 1970 and 57.1% in 1982. This gradual decline in the KMA's share of the urban population signals a reduction in its primacy and an increase in the dominance of secondary towns. While much smaller in aggregate, several secondary towns grew at a faster rate than the KMA. Five secondary centres with populations over 15,000 grew on average by 5.3% from 1970 to 1982. The annual growth rate of the KMA on the other hand was 0.85% from 1970 to 1982. The slowing in the rate of decline of Kingston and the increase in the rate of growth of St Andrew have combined to effect an annual growth rate between 1982 to 1991 of just over 1% for the KMA (Statistical Institute of Jamaica, 1995).

While the decline in the rate of urban growth of the KMA played an important role in the urban strategy not being implemented as envisaged, there were other factors which also had an impact on the strategy. These and other issues concerning the implementation of the strategy will be discussed in the remainder of this chapter.

Portmore

Fifteen miles south-west of Kingston lies Portmore consisting of the communities of Old Portmore, Greater Portmore and Braeton. From the early 1900s a few residents had been living in small communities such as Newlands, Naggo Head, Gregory Park and Old Braeton. They were mostly farmers, fishermen and plantation workers. The main link to the rest of Jamaica at that time was via trains, which passed through Gregory Park. The proposal to develop the area was put forward by the Portmore Land Development Company Limited in the mid-1960s as a means of taking some of the 'overspill' from the ever increasing population of Kingston. It is of interest to note that the principals of this company were also the principals of the Foreshore Development Corporation which was set up to construct Newport West. As stated by the Company, the development was supposed to do three things: relieve extreme housing pressures, particularly in western Kingston; provide for the urbanisation of the agricultural population of south St Catherine; and relieve the government of the cost of opening the Hellshire Hills themselves.

The land in its then state was unusable for three reasons. First, when the Rio Cobre was in spate, the water deluged the low lying areas of what is now known as Portmore. Engineers were called in to design a protective structure to secure the area. Their solution was the construction of a flood-way contained by eleven miles of dyke capable of carrying 73,000 cubic feet per second of flood water. The second problem with Portmore was the distance by road from the industrial and commercial areas of downtown Kingston. To solve this problem the company constructed a three-mile causeway across Kingston Harbour, linking the proposed development to Newport West. The third problem concerned a section of the 809 hectare site created by Portmore which was too low above sea level for construction and required filling. Lands in Portmore were therefore reclaimed through dredging (Matalon, 1990).

The basic structure plan for what is now known as Old Portmore is divided into sectors, each connected to the other by roadways. The development area was set up with water, sewerage and roads laid out by the principal developers, Portmore Land Development Company Limited, so that secondary developers could come in and establish housing schemes with the attendant services and facilities. The sectors were all residential in nature except for the town centre and Waterford, Bridgeport, Westbay and Bayside. The first three were residential and commercial and Bayside was industrial and commercial. The major roadway pattern consisted of a system of major arterials which linked the sectors and from these a series of subdivision roads serviced the development in the sectors. Within each subdivision, the secondary developer had to set up his own road system to facilitate the housing development.

In 1969, the first housing scheme was erected by West Indies Home Contractors (WIHCON) using the pre-cast system of construction. The scheme, Independence City, consisted of 1,373 two- and three-bedroom units. Edgewater Villas, consisting of 689 three-bedroom units, was built by WICHON almost immediately after the completion of Independence City. The construction of Bridgeport, phases 1 and 2, took place between 1972 and 1974. Passage Fort followed in 1974, Waterford in 1975 and Bridgeport, phase 3, in 1976. Portsmouth was built in 1978 and Southboro followed in 1979. In the 1980s the schemes of Westchester, Cumberland and Westbay, phases 1 and 2, were constructed bringing to a close the major developments in Old Portmore. The 1990s saw the construction of Westbay, phase 3, and Bridgeview, and 179 units at Cumberland in 1995. By 1995, it was estimated that the number of housing units in Old Portmore had risen to 16,000, from 534 in 1970, and the population stood at 72,222.

The development at Portmore was originally envisaged as a new town and thus allow for the planned decentralisation of the urban growth taking place in the Kingston Metropolitan Area. However, these plans did not materialise as intended and Old Portmore became nothing more than a planned dormitory satellite of Kingston. While the increase in the number of dwelling units in Portmore helped to ease the chronic housing shortage in the KMA, it was not accompanied by a similar increase in urban services and infrastructure. The lack of adequate facilities and the complaints thereof led the UDC to begin operations in Portmore in 1977. In that year the government instructed the UDC to plan and implement in collaboration with WIHCON the first stage of a programme of social facilities. Since then two neighbourhood centres have been completed: Bridgeport and Waterford. Between them these two centres provide two secondary schools, three primary schools, three infant schools, two police stations, two post offices, a branch library, two community centres, a small medical centre, a health centre and two dental clinics. In addition,

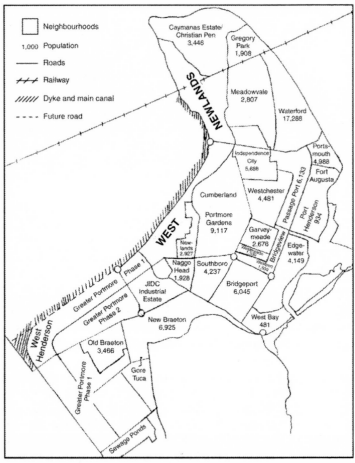

Figure 4.19: Portmore before the construction of the 10,000 units at Greater Portmore. Portmore was originally conceived as a new town, but has become Kingston's largest dormitory satellite.

the UDC owns approximately fifty hectares of land in Portmore on which a civic centre consisting of administrative buildings, a courthouse, a town hall, government offices, public library, health centre, transportation centre and a market are to be constructed on 16.5 hectares. The UDC has also earmarked part of its land reserve for industrial and commercial development.

In 1989, the newly elected Government announced a plan to build 10,000 houses as part of the Greater Portmore scheme. The development of Greater Portmore actually involved the construction of some 16,000 housing units on approximately 1,300 acres of land adjacent to Old Portmore. The first component of the development involved the construction of 10,000 houses in two phases at West Henderson, the new township developed by WIHCON. Eight hundred three-bedroom units and 3,400 two-bedroom units have been constructed. However, the main emphasis of the development has been the construction of 5,800 studio units. The studio or quadraminium is a fully expandable studio developed by WIHCON in response to rising housing costs experienced during the 1980s. The initial unit which the homeowner purchased consisted of a kitchen, a bathroom and one room. The overall size of the unit being twelve by eighteen feet. The unit, however, was designed to permit expansion by the owner as he is able to afford to do so. The units were constructed in clusters, all with two adjacent sides free-standing to allow for expansion. Each unit was sited on its own lot of land, measuring 1,200 square feet. Designs were prepared and made available to show the techniques for expansion. These plans were engineered and approved by the St Catherine Parish Council so that the burden and expense would be taken away from the home owner. WIHCON also prepared bills of quantities for these expansions, so that there would be no doubt about the amount of material that would be required to carry out the expansions.

The expansion plans were prepared so that additions could take place in stages. First a bedroom, and then a second bedroom. There was also an expansion that would have immediately created a two-bedroom house. By doing this WIHCON was attempting to provide an ease of expansion for those whom they thought would be baffled by construction techniques. However, while some home owners utilised the designs provided by WIHCON, a large number undertook construction based on their own plans. Some of these extensions were extremely elaborate and in some instances illegal as they were not approved by the St Catherine Parish Council. In addition to the 10,000 WIHCON houses, the National Housing Trust (NHT) was involved in a joint venture arrangement with the National Housing Corporation (NHC) and the Caribbean Housing and Finance Corporation (CHFC) for the provision of 2,332 additional units.

The major source of funding for the project, US $100 million, came from an arrangement with the Venezuelan and Mexican Governments to use funds under the San Jose Accord to finance development projects. Under this arrangement, the Government of Jamaica was allowed to defer for fifteen years the American dollar debt incurred with the purchase of oil, and was due to be paid in June 1990. The Jamaican dollars, on deposit, were converted into loans for development projects, the first of which was the Greater Portmore scheme. Other funding sources included the NHT, the Commonwealth Development Corporation and the Government of Jamaica. For its provision of financing for the project the NHT received 2,125 studios, 1,256 two-bedroom units and 290 three-bedroom units – a total of 4,000 units for its contributors. The remaining 6,000 units were sold on the open market with CHFC providing mortgage financing for successful applicants.

The announcement of the Greater Portmore development raised some concerns. Foremost were the environmental concerns linked to development in the area. It was felt that sewage disposal in Old Portmore was grossly inadequate and putting an additional 40,000 persons in the area would create even more problems for the already stressed environment. A coastal management study conducted by scientists from the University of the West Indies in 1990 found that the Flashes (wetlands) and the Great Salt Pond were already generating nutrient rich water which was disturbing the ecological balance. They recommended that a system be devised to remove nutrients from sewage effluent and ensure that these nutrients be disposed of away from the Hellshire coastal environment. It had been determined that pollution levels in the

Flashes were above normal because the Braeton treatment plant in Old Portmore was inadequate. In response to these concerns and in order to satisfy the government that the project would not increase the current pollution levels reaching the Flashes, WIHCON hired a group of consultants to undertake an environmental impact assessment of the project. The consultants recommended the construction of approximately forty-one hectares of wetlands to provide tertiary level sewage treatment. WIHCON decided to incorporate the outflow from the Braeton treatment plant in the new system. The sewage is screened and solids settled before it is stabilised in a series of facultative ponds which have become a man-made habitat for crocodiles and birds.

Also high on the list of environmental concerns was the possible liquefaction of the area. As a large part of Portmore is constructed on reclaimed lands concerns were raised on the grounds of the possibility of a disaster brought on by earthquake or storm surge. The developers pointed out, however, that based on studies conducted for Kingston Harbour, Greater Portmore was outside of the liquefaction area. This was demarcated as being

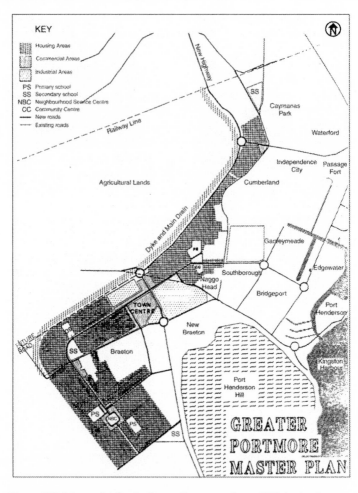

Figure 4.20: Master plan for the Greater Portmore scheme. With its development, Portmore has become the largest single residential community in Jamaica and the second largest in the Caribbean.

nearly three kilometres from Kingston Harbour or 2.4 kilometres from the ocean at Hellshire. In addition, the developers indicated that the greater portion of the development is outside of the reach of the Rio Cobre even if it were to flow over its dykes (Matalon, 1990).

The provision of infrastructure was also another major area of concern. The lack of an adequate supply of water has been a recurring problem in Portmore for many years and in order to meet the projected demand generated by the new development the National Water Commission put a number of new systems in place. These included the purchase and leasing of existing wells, the extension and expansion of lines from existing sources and a major leak detection programme. Inadequate public transportation and traffic congestion on the causeway was another problem cited why the project should not go ahead. The government responded by providing funds to construct and improve highways linking the development to Kingston and Spanish Town. Traffic congestion still remains a problem and plans are being considered to construct a second causeway.

Unlike Old Portmore, the design of Greater Portmore incorporated all the social infrastructure required for a development of this size. Sites were designated for schools, a town centre, neighbourhood shopping, a post office, a police station and a health centre. An existing factory complex for light manufacturing at Naggo Head has also been integrated into the development. To date all these facilities have been completed with the exception of the town centre.

Portmore is now the fastest growing urban centre in Jamaica. It contains several educational institutions, including a national training centre for building skills, the Portmore Heart Academy. The area has several shopping plazas catering for a wide variety of stores and international fast food chains and Portmore has become an important regional shopping centre for the communities of nearby Spanish Town. In an effort to provide much needed employment in Portmore a digiport centre is to be constructed and will generate 3,000 to 3,500 jobs. Construction of the 164,000 square feet of space will be in four stages with the first building to be completed in the latter part of 2001.

While the construction of Portmore has been a significant achievement for the country, the development still has some way to go before its original objectives, that of a new town, are fulfilled. Portmore's rapid population growth over the past twenty-two years has not been matched with infrastructure support and economic activity. There is a need for more investment which would create labour intensive employment and help ease the unemployment situation and the dependence on Kingston as the employment centre for Portmore. The development of the industrial estate at Naggo Head has been slow due to poor access to the port and the proximity of the well-developed industrial complex at Newport East and West in Kingston. Action will have to be taken to encourage investment at Naggo Head. The encouragement of economic activity in the area would help reduce some of the socio-economic pressures being experienced and would also alleviate the transportation problems. The relative lack of employment in Portmore and the need to travel to Kingston have created heavy congestion of traffic on the Portmore Causeway during morning and evening rush hours.

In addition, the rapid growth of the area has not followed any coordinated, long-term strategic development plan. As a consequence, Portmore experiences inadequate urban infrastructure and services, a deteriorating environment and a general lack of employment opportunities. Residents, through their various citizens associations, have pointed to the lack of employment opportunities in the area; the inadequacy and inefficiency of the transportation service; the inadequacy of the health services; inefficient solid waste management practices; lack of recreational and open space facilities; inefficient drainage management; and lack of properly maintained sewage disposal systems. These problems have arisen because of the limited capacity of the local authority to influence and participate in settlement management in the Portmore area. Located at the south-east corner of the parish of St Catherine, far away from the parish capital and more closely allied to Kingston, the provision of basic services such as garbage collection and maintenance of roads and drains by the parish council of Portmore is made even more difficult.

The deteriorating conditions in Portmore have led to a situation where the citizens are demanding that they should be involved in the settlement management processes of their community.

New Strategies for Urban Management

As we saw in Chapter II the political organisation of Jamaica is based on a two-tier system of central and local government. The full array of governmental functions may be found, at a national level, vested in the executive, legislative and judicial branches of national government. In contrast, the local authorities are mainly executive and regulatory agencies. The councils are the only organised governmental political institutions at a local level. There is no decentralised political unit at the town level.

The Joint Portmore Citizens Association (formed from all citizens' associations in the area) set its goal as municipal status for Portmore and in 1994 began to lobby for Portmore to become a municipality. The government in recognising the need for policy shifts that give emphasis to new forms of partnerships and cooperation in the development, operation and maintenance of human settlements, agreed in 1977 to grant municipal status to Portmore. In order to proceed with the establishment of Portmore as a municipality, a Municipality Development Committee was established by the Joint Portmore Citizens Association. This was seen as necessary as there are a number of complex issues to be resolved, such as the institutional and legal framework. Currently, the two-tier system of government does not accommodate the proposed municipality of Portmore as there is no existing geographic location to which municipality status could be conferred. Portmore is not a parish and the parish is the only form of jurisdictional power recognised in law at a local government level. New strategies will have to be determined to facilitate other forms of urban management within the current parish structure of local government. In this regard, the municipality development committee has established five Subcommittees: economic viability to look at the economic base of Portmore to determine if the resources are available to sustain a municipality; legal framework to examine the options of creating a municipality within the St Catherine Parish Council; amenities and services to determine the services and infrastructure for the efficient functioning of the municipality; public education to conduct a programme of public education on municipal status; and local planning committee to set up a local planning authority.

Offices for the local planning authority were recently established and the authority has started operations. The action of the Joint Portmore Citizens Association has indicated to the national government the importance of systematically addressing the need for a dynamic and responsive implementation of an orientated and participatory development planning process. Central government is anticipating therefore, that the outcome of the deliberations in Portmore will form the basis for providing new forms of urban management for the major towns in the country.

Hellshire New Town

The Hellshire Hills, a peninsula twenty-four kilometres to the west of Kingston in the parish of St Catherine consists of 116.5 square kilometres of rolling limestone. They extend from the Great Salt Pond in the east to Salt Creek in the west and rise from the coast to an elevation of nearly 244 metres. They border the sea on the south and on the north adjoin the large agricultural estates which separate the area by eight kilometres from Spanish Town, the parish capital. Hellshire's development was predicated on the potential it presented for relieving the urban pressures of the capital city, Kingston. The primary development objectives of Hellshire were: to provide additional housing areas for the rapidly expanding population of the Kingston and Spanish Town region; to provide first class beaches to serve as the main public recreational area within the region; and to provide job opportunities based on tourist resort development and service industries. The designated area of 10,927 hectares is owned by the UDC and the proposal was to develop 6,070 hectares of flat lands into three self-contained communities; Hellshire Bay New Town, Manatee Bay and Central Highlands New Town. The remainder of the designated area is zoned for conservation, forest reserve and recreational open space.

The development is planned for two phases. The first new town, Hellshire Bay, is projected to provide housing for 60,000 persons and development is currently underway. Manatee Bay which is projected to provide housing for 45,000 to 60,000 persons is slated for development at a later stage. There are no immediate plans at this time to commence development of Central Highlands New Town. The population of the planned residential communities of Hellshire Bay and Manatee Bay is projected to amount to 105,000 to 120,000 if the Hellshire development materialises according to current plans.

Hellshire Bay, encompassing 282 hectares, is to be developed in three phases. Phases 1 and 2 are expected to accommodate approximately 45,000 persons in 6,050 units. The third stage is expected to bring the population up to 60,000. Phases 1 and 2 of the Hellshire Bay New Town is the Hellshire Park Estate. Half of the 6,000 houses in Phases 1 and 2 are contained within the estate. Currently the development is in its initial stages. To date 600 units have been constructed at Cave Hill, Hellshire Heights, Hellshire Park Estates and Seaforth Housing Estates. With a household size of four it is estimated that there are approximately 2,400 persons living in Portmore. Quite a bit of activity is taking place in the Johnson Hills subdivision as lot owners are developing units on their lots. UDC has constructed a basic school, a postal agency and 12,000 square feet of retail space.

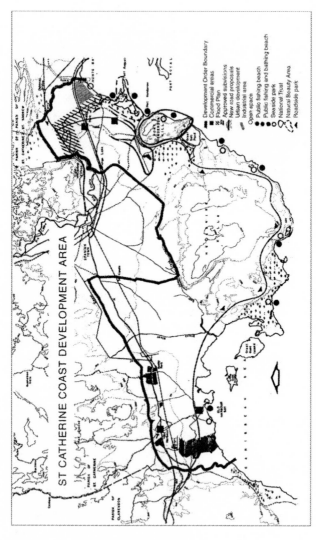

Figure 4.21: South St Catherine Coast Development Order showing the Hellshire Hills. This area is being developed by the Urban Development Corporation in response to population pressures in the KMA.

The development at Hellshire has not proceeded as envisaged as Hellshire has suffered a reduced rate of anticipated housing construction. When the road programme started in 1969, it was projected that all major infrastructure works for the first phase of Hellshire Bay would have been completed by the end of 1976. The land disposal programme commenced in 1975, as first phase areas for disposal became available with access for development blocks created by the road programme. It was projected that secondary development would have commenced by the end of 1976 coinciding with the completion of the first phase infra-structure programme. It was assumed also that the building programme of Hellshire Bay at a building rate of 1,000 units per year would continue unabated for ten years (Hellshire Hills Development Project, UDC Seminar, 1975).

The pace of settlement development in Hellshire has been substantially reduced as a result of the development taking place in Portmore. Growth has also been slow because of the chronic shortage of a dependable water supply, the absence of employ-ment opportunities and limited access. However, environmental considerations have probably acted as the main constraint to the development of the area. The Hellshire coastline is varied, with sheltered white sand bays alternating with rugged cliffs. Much of the shoreline is occupied by mangroves and saline and freshwater swamps with some sandy beaches on the south-east shoreline. The area is also valuable because its relatively inaccessible terrain provides a unique sanctuary for rare plants and animals inhabiting the dry climate of the limestone uplands. As early as 1964, when the St Catherine Coast Development Order was promulgated, the Hellshire Hills were envisaged as an area of national parks, nature reserves, fishing beaches, public beaches and scenic drives. It was also anticipated that some 'resort, residential and related uses' would be provided for after further details were carried out.

However, a decision of the government in 1969 designated the area for development as a new town by the Urban Development Corporation so as to relieve pressures of urban growth in Kingston. Based on the economic evaluation of alternative forms of future urban structure in the Kingston region completed in 1972, the development concept which focused on Hellshire was

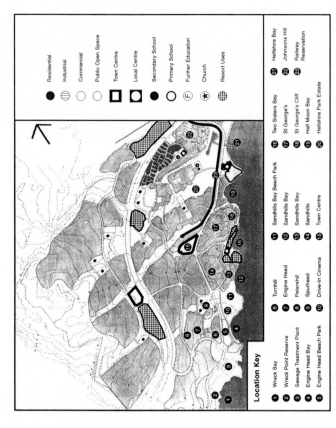

Location Key

1. Wreck Bay
2. Wreck Point Reserve
3. Sewage Treatment Plant
4. Engine Head Bay
5. Engine Head Beach Park
6. Turnhill
7. Engine Head
8. Petershill
9. Spurhead
10. Drive-In Cinema
11. Sandhills Bay Beach Park
12. Sandhills Bay
13. Sandhills Bay
14. Sandhills
15. Town Centre
16. Two Sisters Bay
17. St George's
18. St George's Cliff
19. Half Moon Bay
20. Hellshire Park Estate
21. Hellshire Bay
22. Johnsons Hill
23. Railway Reservation

Symbol	Legend
●	Residential
⊜	Industrial
○	Commercial
○	Public Open Space
□	Town Centre
◻	Local Centre
●	Secondary School
○	Primary School
Ⓕ	Further Education
✴	Church
▦	Resort Uses

Figure 4.22: Hellshire Bay New Town, the first new town being developed by the UDC in Hellshire Hills and which is projected to provide housing for 60,000 persons.

Figure 4.23: Advertisement for housing in one of the schemes developed by the UDC in Hellshire Bay, the first new town being created by the UDC in the Hellshire Hills.

153

selected. This alternative was probably chosen because at Hellshire the government already owned the land, although the economic evaluation revealed that nothing would have been lost in terms of economic efficiency if urban development was concentrated in an urban belt extending from Spanish Town to Old Harbour.

However, by the mid-1970s the ecological sensitivity of the area was being debated. Four areas of concern directly related to the Hellshire Hills development were identified as: the Great Salt Pond; sewage disposal; green belt and open spaces; and the use of Long Pond for recreational purposes. In addition, concerns were expressed about the dislocation of the fishermen at Hellshire Bay, Half Moon Bay and Wreck Beach. The UDC commissioned scientists at the UWI to conduct a study on the ecological resource base of the area. Based on this report, the UDC modified its original plans and reduced the extent of the area to be urbanised so that most of the western sector would remain in its natural state. It is, however, doubtful that the development will materialise as envisaged.

Summary

The planned efforts at decentralisation and redevelopment by the government have not materialised as envisaged and have not been as successful as the activities which have been private sector led. The redevelopment of the Kingston waterfront has not acted as a stimulus for renewal in the surrounding areas. Redevelopment of the downtown area will continue to be problematic as the CBD is no longer at the centre of the city, but is located at a peripheral position in relation to the new suburbs. In addition, the change in the location of commercial activity to a number of outlying centres along the major lines of communications or in new housing developments poses the greatest threat to redevelopment of the downtown. These outlying commercial centres have undermined the importance of the CBD. The supremacy of the CBD as an office centre has also been seriously threatened by the development of a subsidiary office centre in New Kingston which has become the main financial district of the city. The tax incentive programme (TIP) as the main means of stimulating inner city renewal is moving slower than anticipated. It is no doubt being affected by the factors mentioned in addition to the slow down in investment activity in the economy and the method through which the tax incentive is applied.

Planned decentralisation has also not achieved the targets anticipated. This has been due in large measure to a reduction in primacy of the Kingston Metropolitan Area, as the secondary towns and cities grew at a faster rate than the capital city during the period of 1970 to 1990. In addition the plans to set up a series of new towns in Hellshire were stymied somewhat by the rapid growth of Portmore into a major residential satellite of the KMA. Proximity to the KMA and better access made Portmore more attractive for development when compared with Hellshire. In addition, population increase was accommodated in an urban belt extending from Spanish Town to May Pen. In fact this development concept which emerged was recommended in the 1970s as being the most suitable alternative to development in Hellshire. While both alternatives received identical benefit:cost ratios, Hellshire was selected as the development option to be pursued. The major factor influencing this decision was that the land was in government ownership and had already been designated by the government for urban development. Hellshire also appeared attractive to urban development because of the poor soil type which is unsuitable for agriculture due to perennial low rainfall and because of its proximity to the KMA. However, the problem of providing a reliable domestic water supply, the lack of local employment opportunities and the limited access to Kingston via the causeway continue to impose constraints on the projected development of this area.

Although Portmore's growth exceeded planned targets and it still remains a dormitory satellite, there is the potential for new management structures to emerge. The desire of residents in the area to have some say in the management of their community has increased the recognition of the need to broaden the range of relationships between the public, private and community sectors. This recognition for greater coordination has also led to a search for more flexible models of local government management. The introduction of new structures in Portmore would provide the basis for long-term reform of the current local government system and provide a model for the management of other towns and cities in the country.

Figure 2.6: Many of the informal settlements in Kingston are located along the banks of gullies. These sites often pose health and safety hazards caused by pollution and flooding.

Figure 2.7a: Infilling in the Kingston Metropolitan Area by the private sector: apartment complex constructed on former large lot and overlooked by wealthy housing on the hills.

Figure 2.7b: This photograph shows infilling by the public sector townhouses in Mona Heights.

Figure 2.8: A typical colonial house on Duke Street in the north-eastern sector of the eighteenth century grid now occupied by the Jamaica National Heritage Trust.

Figure 2.9: Squatter housing typical of the type found in Trench Town in the 1960s.

Figure 2.10a: An original Mona House. The 680 units which cost US$6,000 each when first offered are now valued upwards of US$125,000.

Figure 2.10b: An aerial view of Mona Heights, the earliest housing scheme constructed in 1958 by WICHON.

Figure 4.1: The Office Centre building in the new Kingston Waterfront with tree-lined avenues and the new highway, Ocean Boulevard.

Figure 4.4: Small commercial establishments in the Kingston Waterfront Project with modern efficient buildings sited around a main entranceway leading to opening courtyards and offices on the second floor.

Figure 4.5a: This photograph shows the Kingston Waterfront Redevelopment Project with one of the new office complexes, the Office Centre and improved parking provided by the development.

Figure 4.5b: This photograph shows the derelict buildings immediately behind the redeveloped waterfront.

Figure 4.6: Constant Spring Road, one of the main uptown shopping plazas with its attractive surroundings and clean modern buildings.

Figure 4.7: Downtown Kingston presents a sharp contrast to conditions in uptown areas when compared with Figure 4.6.

Figure 4.8: One of the worst slums in the city of Kingston is found just north of the Waterfront Redevelopment Project in Central Kingston. It is one of the oldest parts of the city and is characterized by dilapidated buildings and poor infrastructure.

Figure 4.10: Public Buildings West, King Street restored by KRC to house three Goverment Departments.

Figure 4.13: Construction in New Kingston in 1976 with one of the tallest buildings in the area in the background. Restrictions on heights of buildings were lifted in the 1970s allowing the approval of taller structures.

Figure 4.14a(top) and Figure 4.14b(bottom): New Kingston in 1999 showing the development of the area as an office centre. The area is characterized by the predominance of high rise office buildings and the absence of residential and recreational uses.

Figure 4.17: The growth of informal housing in Ocho Ríos is in response to that town's importance as a tourism centre and the formal housing market not being able to provide sufficient housing to cope with the influx of migrants.

Chapter V

NATIONAL PHYSICAL PLANNING

Although the Town Planning Department had produced several development orders since it was established in 1957, it had not until 1963 been involved in the preparation of comprehensive development plans. As we saw in Chapter III, development orders are the legal instruments through which development control regulations are applied to areas of the island for which development orders have been prepared. In April 1963, J Stanley Ott, an expert in physical planning provided through USAID, was attached to the Town Planning Department on a three-month mission and prepared a report entitled 'Report on the St Andrew – St Catherine Planning Region'. This report was circulated to various interested bodies and organisations but resulted in very little direct action at the time. However, in early 1963 the Government of Jamaica approached the United Nations to request the services of a physical planner for a period of twelve months to assist and advise the Town Planning Department in establishing a methodology for the collection, analysis and presentation of physical planning data for the preparation of regional plans; applying this methodology in the preparation of regional plans; and preparing a set of proposals for the administrative arrangements for the implementation and execution of such plans. The expert, Professor TJ Manickam commenced his assignment in September 1965 and completed it in November 1966. His final report entitled *Clarendon Regional Plan* contained a set of recommendations for the future physical development of the parish of Clarendon.

During his stay in Jamaica, Professor Manickam was also instrumental in assisting with the preparation of a request from the Government of Jamaica to the special fund of the United Nations Development Program (UNDP) for a new project entitled Assistance in Physical Development Planning. This project was approved by the governing council of the Special Fund in January 1967. The UN was appointed as the executing agency and the project commenced in April 1967 with the arrival of the first expert who became the project manager, WP Paterson. The plan of operation of the project was signed on 9 May, 1968 and was declared operational as of 14 May, 1968. The purpose of the project, the duration of which was four years, was to assist the Government of Jamaica through the Town Planning Department of the Ministry of Finance and Planning in the preparation of national, regional and local physical development plans for Jamaica and to make adequate provision for, and to assist in the training of Jamaican personnel in these techniques.

In this chapter we will examine the scope, content and recommendations of the first National Physical Plan of 1970 to 1990. Then we will turn to the second National Physical Plan of 1978 to 1998 as we compare that document with the first National Physical Plan, and try to sum up the effect of these documents on planning in Jamaica.

National Physical Plan 1970–1990

BACKGROUND FOR PLANNING

Scope and Content
The scope and purpose of the first National Physical Plan for Jamaica was to present a series of guidelines for the long-term physical development of the country. These guidelines were set against the background of the physical resources and constraints, the social and economic conditions of the country and the development trends which were continuously reshaping the physical environment. The National Physical Plan was not intended to be a rigid and finite blueprint to indicate precise locations, forms and timing of all types of development, but rather it sought to set goals, establish planning principles, and above all stress the need for comprehensive approaches to problems of planning and development regardless of whether the issues at stake were of local, regional or national interest (National Physical

Plan 1970–90).

The National Physical Plan carefully tried to set out the differences between 'town planning' which was being practised in the island at that time and the newer concept of 'physical planning' being introduced with the preparation of the National Physical Plan. The National Physical Plan stated this as follows:

> Physical Planning is concerned with the progressive and orderly development of regions, cities, towns and rural areas in order to create a safe, well-balanced and harmonious physical environment within which the individual, his family and the community can enjoy a secure, active, varied and pleasant life. Formerly known as 'Town Planning' this field has assumed a wider significance in recent years as physical planners have become aware of the need to relate town and regional plans to economic and social goals as well as to the protection and preservation of the natural environment.

(National Physical Plan 1971, p.3)

The National Physical Plan pointed out that although physical planning had been legally established in Jamaica in the form of town and country planning since 1957, this concept was not only new to Jamaica but was also a recent concept in the international planning field at that time. It went on to say that although economic and social planning had been undertaken in many developing countries since 1950, it was only in recent years that physical planning had received growing attention as an essential component of the national development process. The National Physical Plan pointed out that there was a growing recognition of the relationship between socio-economic development and physical development. In this regard, economic and social programmes are concerned with activating higher production and a resultant rise in levels of living depend, in part, on some form of physical expression such as industrial estates, schools, highways, housing schemes and the controlled exploitation or conservation of the natural resources of the country. The plan concluded that it is the location, extent, intensity of use and the appropriate relationship of these features to each other which is the special concern of physical planning.

Method of Preparation

In order to identify the major problems which Jamaica would face over the two decades from 1970 to 1990, and to suggest the approaches which should be taken to guide physical development at a national level, the authors of the National Physical Plan of 1970–90 conducted several studies and surveys. Some twenty detailed surveys and substantial reports dealing with a wide variety of subjects were done as background to the summary positions stated in the plan. Every ministry of government was involved in the preparation of the National Physical Plan and in particular, the authors of the plan worked very closely with the Central Planning Unit (CPU). The proposed long-range development strategy as expressed in the five-year plan for 1970–75 prepared by the CPU was used as the starting point for the preparation of the National Physical Development Plan. The strategy was translated into specific physical planning policies within the context of meeting the many existing and anticipated needs of the country. This was seen as essential so that such physical development policies could be integrated with those adopted for economic and social progress so that each policy reinforced the other.

Of major concern was the projection by the CPU that by 1990 the population of Jamaica would be in the region of 2,670,000, (the actual 1990 population was 2.4 million), an increase of about 770,000 persons from 1970 to 1990. It was envisaged that virtually all these additional people would be living in towns and cities, doubling the current urban population. Also, it was anticipated that over the next twenty years (1970–90), rapid economic progress would continue in the major sectors of agriculture, forestry and fisheries, manufacturing, tourism, mining and mineral processing. The plan concluded therefore, that the future increased population, greater urbanisation, expanded economic activities of the country, and rising affluence of Jamaicans, would create great demands for employment; for the full range of public and private services; and especially for land to be developed with housing, work places, commercial establishments, schools, parks, and all the myriad of facilities that would be required to achieve and maintain a good way of life.

Rates of National Population Growth 1943–70 with estimates to 1990

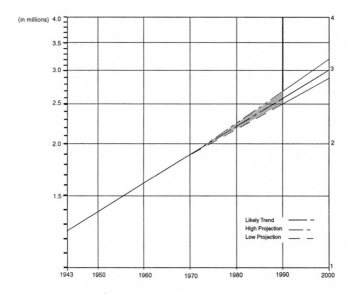

Figure 5.1: The long-term population projections used by the National Physical Plan were made to indicate very broadly the scale of anticipated development needs in Jamaica over the period of 1970-90. The figures were therefore not considered as predictions or firm estimations.

Recommendations

A series of long-term development strategies were formulated in order to offset some of the identified problems. These strategies encompassed the major sectors of the economy and included agriculture, forestry and fisheries; mining; tourism; manufacturing; utilities and social facilities; housing; transportation; parks, recreation and conservation; environmental quality; and urban structure and policy. However, the key components of the plan were agriculture, tourism, manufacturing and the urban structure and policy. Agriculture, tourism and manufacturing were important as they provided the basis on which population projections by parish were made for 1990. The methodological approach used to establish the target 1990 population distribution was the allocation of the labour force projections and land use recommendations of the National Physical Plan. The projections for Kingston, St Andrew and St Catherine were combined because the Plan predicated that these parishes would increasingly tend to function as a single area, especially with respect to commuting from one parish to another. These projections were considered the target projections for the parishes.

In addition, the population growth rate for each parish was extended in a straight line to 1990 to project the same rate of increase as the parishes experienced in the period from 1960 to 1970. However, this trend projection, the plan pointed out, gave only a general indication of the likely distribution of population by parish and did not take into account the anticipated large increase of jobs in tourism in north coast parishes, the proposed distribution of additional industrial acreage recommended in the National Physical Plan and the subsequent implications and influence of these job targets on national population distribution. Table V compares the trend and target projections for each parish with the 1960 and 1970 population figures and also indicates the percentage share of national population held by each parish at the time of the 1960 and 1970 censuses as well as the anticipated shares of the national population which would be held by each parish in accordance with the trend and target projections.

Table V: *Trend and Target Population Projections by Parish, 1990*

Parish	1960 census	% total population	1970 census	% total population	1990			
					Trend	% total population	Target	% total population
St Catherine	572,900	35.6	736,200	39.5	1,309,200	49.0	1,151,500	43.1
Clarendon	164,000	10.2	176,700	9.5	205,700	7.7	208,400	7.8
Manchester	111,800	6.9	123,500	6.6	149,600	5.7	141,600	5.3
St Elizabeth	116,700	7.2	126,600	6.8	149,600	5.7	133,600	5.0
Westmoreland	109,600	6.8	113,200	6.1	141,600	5.3	144,300	5.4
Hanover	53,900	3.3	58,900	3.2	77,500	2.9	98,900	3.7
St James	83,000	5.2	103,700	5.5	155,000	5.8	165,700	6.2
Trelawny	56,100	3.5	61,300	3.3	74,800	2.8	93,500	3.5
St Ann	114,400	7.1	121,100	6.5	141,600	5.3	176,300	6.6
St Mary	94,200	5.9	99,900	5.3	112,200	4.2	138,900	5.2
Portland	64,500	4.0	68,400	3.7	77,500	2.9	106,900	4.0
St Thomas	68,700	4.3	71,400	3.8	77,500	2.9	112,200	4.2
TOTAL	1,609,800	100%	1,861,000	100%	2,671,800	100%	2,671,800	100%

Source: *National Physical Plan*, p.54

The principal differences between these two projections made by the National Physical Planning team were: the containment of the three major parishes of the Kingston region to 43% of the total population if the National Physical Plan recommendations were implemented as opposed to 49% if the present trend continued; and the marked increases in all north coast parishes in the anticipation of meeting the tourism employment targets expressed in the National Physical Plan. The small differences between trend and target populations in the parishes of Clarendon, Manchester and St Elizabeth were as a result of the minor role these parishes were expected to play in the future growth of tourism and the relatively static degree of employment in the bauxite and alumina industry. Generally the two projections demonstrated that the recommendations of the National Physical Plan had envisaged that there would have been a better balanced pattern of the distribution of employment island-wide and a concomitant lessening of population growth pressures on the Kingston region.

Because of the overall importance which agriculture, manufacturing and tourism were to play in the distribution of employment and population, and the urban structure it is useful to briefly examine the policies outlined for these sectors in the National Physical Plan.

Tourism

The major significance of tourism according to the National Physical Plan was its potential for the provision of new jobs, particularly in those areas of Jamaica which had little or no resource base for the continued provision of jobs in agriculture, bauxite or manufacturing. The plan projected that by 1990 approximately 38,500 additional tourist rooms and 65,000 additional jobs in tourism would be created. The need to provide such a large number of jobs over the planning period led to the articulation of a long-term development strategy for tourism by the plan's authors. This strategy was to provide a guide for developers and allow government to plan and coordinate the provision of utilities and services in the most economical manner. Another reason for the location strategy was the need to ensure that development was concentrated as far as possible into compact areas so that large stretches of countryside and coastline would be preserved for recreational, agricultural and conservation uses. The proposed strategy for tourism development divided the island into two zones according to the two tributary areas of the international airports. Zone 1 was characterised largely by its orientation towards the coast and beaches and contained the well-established resort centres of Montego Bay and Ocho Rios. Zone 2, although lacking the beaches of the north coast, has many assets which the Plan pointed out had the potential for development. For example, within Zone 2 lies the 'Triangle of History' (Spanish Town, Kingston and Port Royal).

Certain areas were identified by the Plan as resort centres, in order that both the government and the private sector would channel the complete range of infrastructure and resources into such areas. Other areas identified only as resorts were to have been restricted in size and scope of services. The plan also paid considerable attention to the rural areas and the south coast, neither of which had experienced the impact of tourism received by the north coast. In this regard the plan recommended the continued rapid development of a full range of tourist attractions which reflect the Jamaican landscape and cultural heritage. The Plan further recommended that within the context of regional plans which would further detail the character and extent of the proposed resorts and resort centres, amendments should be made to existing coastal development orders to indicate the priorities of development which should also be related to the staged extension of services and utilities.

Agriculture, Forestry and Fisheries

The plan pointed out that many of the ways to rationalise agriculture related to non-physical factors such as social attitudes, marketing structures, provision of adequate credit and training of farmers in new techniques. While these were beyond the scope of physical planning, the plan intimated that they could be assisted indirectly through physical planning. Underlying the physical development policies for agriculture and forestry is the concept that agricultural development is an integral part of overall rural development which, in turn, is an essential ingredient of the country's total progress. Another important concept presented by

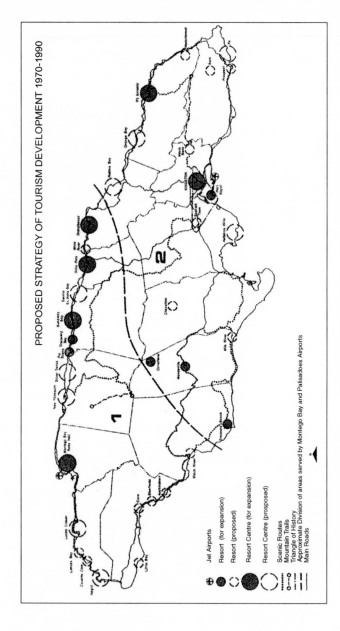

Figure 5.2: The National Physical Plan 1970 to 1990 proposed a specific location strategy for tourism based on two zones in the island. The plan also recommended two general types of tourist facilities, resorts and resort centres.

the plan was that of rationalisation of agriculture and that it be viewed as a type of industry. This approach, the plan indicated, meant that agriculture be provided with industrial-type incentives and maximum efficiency achieved through such changes as mechanisation, specialisation of crop production areas and greatly improved marketing structures. The plan also pointed out the need for specialised research in the area of crop production and irrigation. Against this background the plan proposed development policies for agriculture in the areas of: agricultural zoning; vegetable production for domestic consumption and processing; utilisation of idle lands; reduced use of marginal lands; forestry development; improvement of the land tenure situation; alternative means of employment; preservation of good fishing beaches; development of a major fishing harbour facility in the Kingston region; and upgrading of selected towns and agricultural regions.

Manufacturing

The major policies recommended for the manufacturing sector were the provision of 70,000 additional jobs in manufacturing; the reservation of an additional 810 hectares for further industrial expansion; and the application of an industrial location strategy. The first component of this strategy was the staged development of an industrial region in south-east Jamaica with the primary centre focused on the port facilities in Kingston and secondary centres in the several towns between May Pen and Morant Bay. The second concept of this strategy was the development of a major general manufacturing centre in Montego Bay serving an export market through the freeport and airport and also the domestic market of western and northern Jamaica. The final component of the strategy was the establishment of small industrial estates in all the remaining rural parishes, based primarily on local supplies of raw materials, employment needs and service to local markets.

The general objectives of a national strategy of industrial location were: the provision of industrial sites and estates in such a manner which would have met the island-wide demand for new jobs without necessitating an additional migration to the Kingston Metropolitan Area; diversification of the employment base of the parish capitals and towns of similar size; the creation of new employment opportunities in localities with little or no potential employment in tourism or bauxite industries; and the coordination of industrial development with the parallel development of infrastructure, social services and residential areas.

Urban Structure and Policy

The centrepiece of the National Physical Plan was an urban structure and policy, which was established as the spatial framework to guide socio-economic development so that urbanisation would proceed on a rational basis. It was a clear recognition of the document that the urban hierarchy should be treated as a system, and used as a tool for correcting some of the disparities between Kingston and the rest of the country (Hudson, 1980). The underlying principle of the policy is that urbanisation in itself is not an undesirable result of national development but rather is a natural accompaniment to economic growth and, if guided carefully, can become an important agent for social and economic progress. On this basis, it was determined that there was a need for a clearly articulated urban policy which would be implemented according to an urban structure and specific techniques applied to accomplish the policy. The background to the articulation of an urban structure and policy was as a result of rapid urbanisation which was occurring at that time especially in Kingston and Montego Bay and to a lesser extent in smaller towns. It was projected at that time that rapid urbanisation would continue and that the rural growth of the country would remain static over the next twenty years and that the population increase of approximately 770,000 persons would be virtually all in urban areas.

The urban structure was viewed at that time as the key element in the National Physical Plan because it would synthesise many of the other development policies and would provide the basis for making certain planning decisions. The main objective of the national urban policy was to provide for the comprehensive development of towns and cities throughout the country in order to relieve the population pressures in Kingston, offer a greater choice of urban living environments throughout the country, provide a higher level of services, promote integrated regional development, and provide a guide for the most rational use of

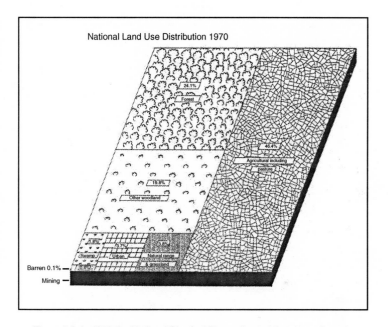

National Land Use Distribution 1970

24.1%
Forest

46.4%
Agricultural including pasture

19.8%
Other woodland

1.8%
Swamp

3.7%
Urban

3.1%
Natural range & grassland

Barren 0.1%

Mining

Figure 5.3: In 1970 the National Physical Plan estimated that approximately 40,500 hectares of land were in urban use. This included land committed to urban use by subdivision into residential or resort lots.

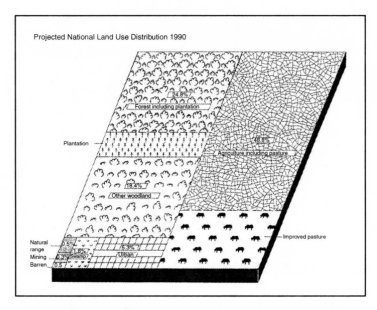

Figure 5.4: Major gross change in land uses from 1970 to 1990 was based on a series of policies which restricted subdivision and further urban development to the minimum intrusions on to good agricultural land and future land needs over the plan period.

public and private investment in urban development (National Physical Plan, 1971).

Determination of the most appropriate urban places to receive development emphasis in the future involved several steps of analysis. Of the existing 1,150 towns and villages, about 215 were selected based on their then size and importance as service centres for the surrounding hinterland and on other development factors such as existing and proposed public facilities as well as proposed economic activities. These 215 towns were then assigned a quantitative ranking according to ten development criteria. The total points received by each town then served as a guide for the final selection with consideration given at that stage to other factors such as physical expansion possibilities, future water supply and the travel-time distance relationship among the towns. The towns selected as the proposed urban structure include five regional centres – Mandeville, Montego Bay, St Ann's Bay, May Pen and Port Antonio, with Kingston performing regional as well as national centre functions – nineteen sub-regional centres and eighty-seven district centres; a total of 112 urban places.

The hierarchy of centres selected was not based on population size or functions, but rather the hierarchy reflected the provision of a minimum of certain services being available at each level of centre in order to provide the urban service function to both town residents and rural inhabitants in the surrounding tributary areas. It was proposed that each regional and sub-regional centre would also provide sub-regional and district town functions. The urban structure which was to provide the spatial framework for future urban development was supported by a number of policy measures designed to achieve the objectives of the national urban policy. These measures included: development and distribution of new sources of employment; balanced development of public infrastructure according to established priorities; development of integrated town centres; and encouragement and incentives given to the private sector to follow the national urban structure and policy (National Physical Plan, 1971).

Plan Implementation

It was stated in the National Physical Plan that implementation of the policies and strategies recommended in the document would depend on the social and economic policies of the government, the location and timing of capital investment by the various ministries concerned with physical development, the cooperation of the parish councils, and the guidance by the appropriate agencies of the government of investment by private corporations and individuals (National Physical Plan, 1971). In order to achieve these objectives the plan recommended an effective national physical planning programme to contain: data collection and processing; preparation and amendment of physical plans; coordination of public sector planning; and guidance of private developers. The plan had envisaged that the task of coordinating public sector planning would be initiated by the Town Planning Department and the department would play a pivotal role in providing advice for the Jamaican tourist board and the Factories Corporation of Jamaica in the location of new investment.

The paradigm shift that was expected to take place with the introduction of a new approach to planning never materialised as anticipated. This was due in part to the fact that the government which came to power in 1972 never officially adopted the National Physical Plan prepared under the previous administration (Hudson, 1980). But despite the plan not really serving the purpose for which it was designed, it did have a significant impact on planning in the country. For the first time, planning ideas and policies were directed at wider issues than development control and the preparation of development orders. Perhaps the most important legacy of the National Physical Plan exercise was the establishment of a unit within the Town Planning Department which was concerned with the preparation of development plans. While development control once again became the major focus of the Town Planning Department's work activities with the National Physical Plan not officially accepted, there was some recognition of this new approach to planning. The plan also had an impact, if only briefly, on the importance attached to planning. The preparation of the plan involved a number of agencies and the resultant policies came out of the interaction of these agencies. Thus, in many ways the policies really reflected the particular concerns and approaches of the technocrats in these agencies and some of the agencies involved in the preparation of the Plan continued to use it as a reference document.

National Physical Plan 1978–1998

SCOPE AND CONTENT

In 1978 the government decided that there should be another National Physical Plan and the Town Planning Department was given the task to prepare a plan for the twenty-year period, 1978 to 1998. What is particularly striking about the National Physical Plan of 1978 to 1998 is the close resemblance it bears to its predecessor, the 1970 to 1990 National Physical Plan. Hudson (1980) points out that the authors of the revised version tried to adopt as much as of the original as possible:

> Because of the scientific way in which the original proposal was developed and also because it is well known in planning sections of various government agencies and underlies many of their plans.

(cited in Hudson, 1980, p.9)

The 1978 to 1998 National Physical Plan also met the same fate as the first plan. A new government elected in 1980 did not implement either of the National Physical Plans as a result of the serious constraints experienced in the economy during the 1980s. Implementation of the plans were stymied as the government sought to introduce corrective measures and economic reform under a structural adjustment programme, although the government did attempt to implement elements of the urban structure through a comprehensive rural township development programme, as we will see in Chapter VI.

The underpinning of the second National Physical Plan was the urban structure and policy, adopted from the first plan, and now referred to as the National Settlement Strategy. The settlement strategy increased the number of urban centres to 120.

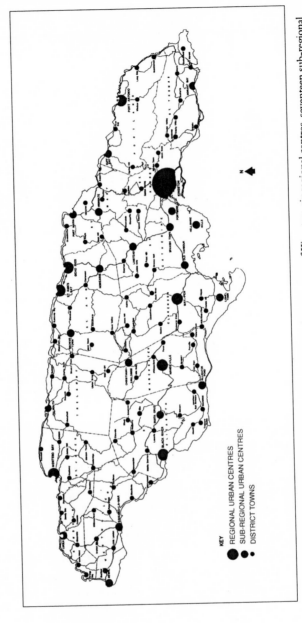

KEY

● REGIONAL URBAN CENTRES
● SUB-REGIONAL URBAN CENTRES
• DISTRICT TOWNS

Figure 5.5: The National Settlement Strategy designated an urban structure of Kingston, six regional centres, seventeen sub-regional centres and ninety-six district centres as the most appropriate urban places to receive development emphasis in the future.

Portmore was included as a regional centre, the number of sub-regional centres was reduced from nineteen to seventeen and nine new district centres were added.

An important element of the 1978 to 1998 plan was the policy of increasing decentralisation. The island was subdivided into six planning regions with a regional centre to serve each region. Each centre selected was supposed to function as the stimulus and focus of regional development and together they were expected to operate as a system of service centres for the entire island. There was also some concern that there was a need to plan for areas larger than parishes which were spatially or environmentally connected and where parishes had a similar economic base. This was the first time the concept of comprehensive planning at a sub-national level other than the parish was introduced.

Although narrower in scope, mention should be made of the division of the country into thirteen regional land authorities in 1969. These land authorities were to provide the framework for integrated planning and development of agriculture. The land authority boundaries were drawn to include areas of geographic homogeneity with administrative centres selected on the basis of their being served with modern facilities including good transport to other towns. Basic concepts of the land authorities were decentralisation of administration and decision making to the local areas and coordinated and integrated application of the several interrelated services and support programmes necessary for comprehensive agricultural development. The programme was modelled on two land authorities, Yallahs Valley and Christiana, which had been operating successfully for several years prior to 1969. As we saw in Chapter IV when a special local planning authority was required for Negril in 1959, the land authority was the mechanism used to confer planning powers under the Town and Country Planning Act to a body which spanned more than one parish.

The division of the island into six planning regions as the mechanism through which regional development would be accomplished met with very little success. The concept was not accepted and from the outset the defined regions were embroiled

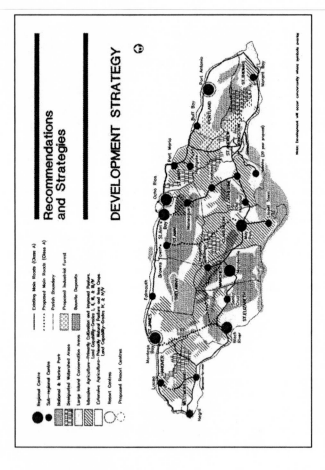

Figure 5.6: The Development Strategy Map indicated in a very general way the combination of the proposals for the various sectors of the economy in relationship to each other as the basis of a comprehensive and integrated strategy for the period of 1978 to 1998.

in controversy as we will see in Chapter VI. In addition, over the two decades since the preparation of the National Physical Plans the concerns of spatial planning have become less influential in national policy decisions leading to the demise of regional planning.

Like the first plan, the National Physical Plan of 1978 to 1998 prepared a Land Use Strategy Map for the projected twenty-year cycle. This map was identical to that in the first plan and reflected to a very large degree the studies and reports prepared by various agencies of the government for the 1970 to 1990 plan. For example, the delineation of the agricultural areas was based on the land capability studies completed by the Ministry of Agriculture and information on bauxite deposits were received from the then Department of Mines.

To a large degree this map was based on the natural resources with which Jamaica is endowed. The map was intended to illustrate a general strategy of long-term land management which would utilise the natural resources of Jamaica in a manner which would facilitate maximum economic benefits while at the same time giving full consideration to the principles of conservation outlined in the report. While it was recognised that there would have been conflicts in reconciling the need for economic development with the need to protect and preserve the natural environment, it was hoped that the development strategy map would eliminate some of these conflicts. It was emphasised, however, that more specific planning policies were required at the regional and local levels and it was expected that this strategy map would assist in formulating these policies by illustrating at a national level the major opportunities, constraints and limitations of development.

Summary

The account above indicates the profound influence politics had on the planning process in the 1970s. Because a National Physical Plan was prepared by one political administration it was not recognised officially by another political administration. Despite this, the first plan set the stage for an understanding that there was a need for a greater emphasis on the spatial and resource aspects of planning than there had been in the past. This understanding led to the preparation of another National Physical Plan eight years later.

Although two National Physical Plans were prepared, the policy shifts that were expected as a result did not occur. The integration of economic planning with spatial planning has not been achieved and the National Settlement Strategy has not been used as a coordinating mechanism as was intended. In fact national urbanisation strategies have tended to operate apart from other social and economic policies. The National Settlement Strategy was essentially designed to allow urbanisation taking place in the country to proceed on a rational basis, but this objective was often in conflict with other sector objectives.

In addition, this new approach to planning was not backed up by legal instruments and statutes. No requirements were put in place for regional plans and local area plans to be prepared and regularly updated. The Town and Country Planning Act was still the legal mechanism for planning and development orders were the statutory provisions required under the Act. Thus, despite an understanding by many planners of the need for decentralised development according to natural resource potential and location advantages, there was some resistance to change.

Chapter VI
REGIONAL PLANNING

Regional planning in Jamaica has had a complex and somewhat confusing history. Introduced in the early 1970s it gained prominence in the late 1970s and since then has declined in importance. It has embraced many doctrines and the gap between theory and practice has in large measure accounted for its disappearance from the planning agenda. As was discussed in Chapter IV, regional planning, as it has been widely practised in Jamaica, is based on the Geddesian concept of the 'natural region' as the basic unit for planning. In this context planning involves whole regions encompassing a number of towns and their surrounding spheres of influence (Hall, 1992).

While most regional planning in Jamaica has been undertaken based on the tradition mentioned above, it has not been the only doctrine which has influenced regional planning in the country. Regional planning was seen also as occupying a middle level of planning between national and local area and/or urban planning. This doctrine of regional planning embraces the vision of integrated development of natural resources for human use in an appropriate unit of sub-national space. This approach adapted from comprehensive river basin development in the United States of America, saw regional plans focusing on the issues and objectives which were more narrow in scope than a national level. It was envisaged that there would be a mutual inter-relationship among national, regional and local area and urban planning with each subsequent one fitting into the framework of the one above with the regional plan forming a bridge between the other two.

The regional plan was seen as forming the framework for the local area or urban plan. It would therefore be prepared in greater detail than the national plan, but not with the preciseness required of the local area or urban plan. Consequently, regional planning was to provide the framework for development on a more manageable level in contrast to the global scale of national planning where strategies tended to be all inclusive and generalised. This form of regional planning with its strong territorial bias also had an important influence on planning practice. The division of the island into planning regions discussed in Chapter V was based on this concept and the form and scope of regional plans in the 1970s and 1980s reflected comprehensive development at a sub-national level.

While the practice of regional planning took the form of the preparation of territorial development plans, this was not the main doctrine of regional planning introduced in the 1970s. Inherent in the urban structure and policy and the National Settlement Strategy, key elements of the first and second National Physical Plans, was the concept of 'growth centres'. This form of regional planning stressed the spatial integration of the national economy based on an urban hierarchy. Growth centres were those urban places that, through a combination of direct investments and capital subsides to enterprises, would bring about the development of the surrounding regions (Friedmann and Weaver, 1979).

In this chapter, therefore, we will first look at the initiatives in regional planning and the process of regional planning in Jamaica. We will then examine the regional problem and the efforts made to try to address the problem through the implementation of regional plans and programmes. Finally the chapter will examine whether there is a need for regional planning in Jamaica.

Regional Planning Initiatives

SPATIAL PLANNING INITIATIVES

National Urban Structure and Policy

The Urban Structure and Policy which was published in 1971 in the first National Physical Plan was the first attempt at regional planning in Jamaica. As we saw in Chapter V, this urban structure was to provide the framework through which the capacity of small and intermediate settlements would be strengthened to generate more widespread and equitable development.

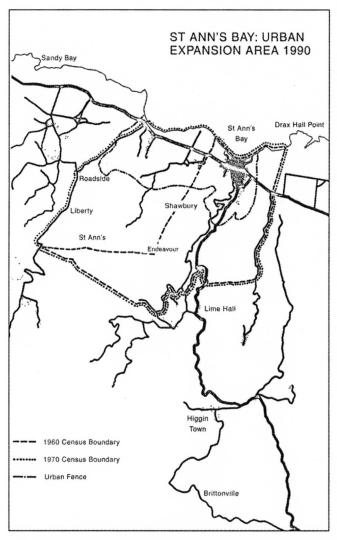

ST ANN'S BAY: URBAN
EXPANSION AREA 1990

Sandy Bay

St Ann's
Bay

Drax Hall Point

Roadside

Shawbury

Liberty

St Ann's

Endeavour

Lime Hall

Higgin
Town

- - - 1960 Census Boundary

•••••••• 1970 Census Boundary

—•—•— Urban Fence

Brittonville

Figure 6.1: The North Coast Regional Development Plan established 'urban
fences' for nine north coast towns in order to limit town expansion
and runaway approval of subdivisions which had little
bearing on current development of the town.

Regional Plans

Within the general framework of the 1970 to 1990 National Physical Plan more detailed urban and regional plans were to be produced. The first such plan was the North Coast Regional Plan which was prepared by the Physical Planning Unit of the Town Planning Department of the Ministry of Mining and Natural Resources under the UNDP project, Assistance in Physical Planning in May 1972. The framework of the plan was based on the National Physical Plan but offered more details in location of employment and detailing the urban structure, particularly in regard to determining urban fences for the fast-growing towns in the region. It was deemed necessary to draw boundaries around urban centres in order to maximise public investment by establishing more stringent controls on urban development. The main rationale for this action was the large number of subdivisions which had been approved mainly for speculative purposes and considered premature as they bore no relationship to the development of the town. As was the case with the National Physical Plan, this plan received very little support.

The Kingston Regional Plan, published in 1973, was the second regional plan prepared. This regional plan was prepared so as to bring order and purpose to the development of the Kingston region. As was discussed in Chapter IV, the selection of the alternative form of urban structure appears to have been an over-ambitious attempt to decentralise urban growth in the Kingston region.

National Settlement Strategy

The Urban Structure and Policy was succeeded by the National Settlement Strategy (NSS) in the National Physical Plan published in 1978. The objectives were similar to those outlined in the Urban Structure and Policy. However, neither have been used as a tool for correcting some of the disparities between Kingston and the rest of the country. The NSS is used mainly by the Town Planning Department as the basis for refusing development applications when these developments fall outside of the urban centres included in the National Settlement Strategy. Developers are reminded that the *Manual for Development* points out that they should be aware of the strategy as it provides the spatial framework for future urban development and is part of the methodology for achieving a rational pattern of land use and community development. Cognisance of this policy the manual states, will benefit developers in that they will be aware of where investment would be most productive from their perspective. However, the strategy has not guided various governments' investment in infrastructure or the development of integrated town centres as was intended.

Planning Regions

The 1978 to 1998 National Physical Plan proposed the division of the island into six planning regions in order to encourage regional development. However, the concept faced serious opposition. The first problem was concern over how the regions were demarcated. Regions were made up of parishes grouped together on the basis of certain criteria. These criteria included factors such as geographic and ecological similarities; location of a regional centre in each region; similarity of economic activities and level of economic development; and similar cultural practices. While most regional boundaries followed parish boundaries there were some instances where this was not the case. For example, the eastern half of the parish of St Mary with its tourism activities was considered as being more closely allied to the tourism parish of St Ann and was therefore included in the St Ann–St Mary region. On the other hand, the eastern half of St Mary with its banana plantations was included within the agricultural parish of Portland in what was considered as a rural Portland–St Mary region. Similarly, the western portion of Westmoreland was included in the tourism dominated St James–Hanover–Trelawny region because the major tourism destination of Negril stretches across the parishes of Hanover and Westmoreland.

As these boundaries did not follow the traditional parish boundaries the regions were considered unacceptable administrative units by the ministries and agencies responsible for implementing government programmes and projects. The northern boundary of the Manchester–Clarendon region was a particularly contentious boundary as it did not follow the Manchester–Trelawny parish boundary or the St Ann–Clarendon parish boundary. The boundary encompassed all the agricultural

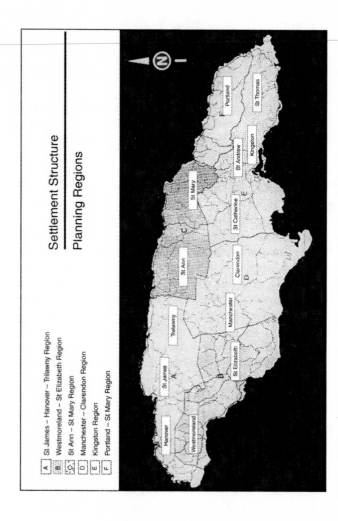

Settlement Structure

Planning Regions

A	St James – Hanover – Trelawny Region
B	Westmoreland – St Elizabeth Region
C	St Ann – St Mary Region
D	Manchester – Clarendon Region
E	Kingston Region
F	Portland – St Mary Region

Figure 6.2: The 1978 to 1998 National Physical Plan divided the island into six planning regions in response to the growing awareness of the problems of regional imbalance and over-concentration of population and development in the capital region.

communities in the upper reaches of the Rio Minho which had similar farming practices and which were included in the former Christiana Area Land Authority. While the boundary was acceptable when directed specifically to agricultural development, it was viewed as unsuitable in a wider context which had management implications.

The administrative functions of the planning regions also created problems. When the idea of a regional division was first suggested by the Town Planning Department in 1973, it was envisaged that there would be some form of administration in place to manage the region. The national government, however, dismissed the notion of a third level of government very early on the grounds that it was beyond the financial capacity of the country and would require major constitutional changes. Some form of a regional coordinating body was proposed, but its form and functions were never clearly set out on paper. In addition the Kingston Regional Plan had proposed the establishment of a Kingston Regional Planning Council to direct, coordinate and implement the planning and development of the Kingston region. Such a council was never set up despite the detailing of the structure, powers and responsibilities and role of the council in the Kingston Regional Plan.

Because of these issues, the National Physical Plan of 1978 to 1998 stressed the concept of regions being used for planning purposes rather than for the introduction of a new form of governance. The plan recommended that development in the country be pursued within the context of the six planning regions defined by the Town and Country Planning Department and the settlement strategy (National Physical Plan, 1978). It was proposed therefore that the Ministry of Finance would ensure that development plans and projects submitted by the various development ministries and agencies were complementary to each other and that planned implementation was coordinated. This proposal for sub-national coordination using the Town Planning Department's six planning regions also ran into another set of problems. Ministries and agencies implementing programmes on a regional basis objected to these regions on the grounds that they had defined other regions which better suited their objectives. In most instances the major objection raised was in connection with the boundaries used to demarcate the regions.

ECONOMIC PLANNING INITIATIVES

National and Regional Planning

In 1972 there was a major reorganisation of the planning system. The reorganisation of the Central Planning Unit into the National Planning Agency had a direct impact on regional planning. Ministry Paper no. 10 tabled in the House on 10 May 1972 set out the organisational structure for economic and social planning (Bonnick, 1995). The Economic Council made up of core ministers and chaired by the Prime Minister was responsible for policy. A technical advisory committee made up of individuals from academia and the public and private sectors provided comment on development policy when required and also advised the National Planning Agency on its draft plans and research projects. The National Planning Agency was the technical secretariat to the Economic Council. A number of consultative committees were also set up with membership from the public and private sectors (Bonnick, 1995).

In order to carry out this and other functions under a reorganised national planning framework the National Planning Agency was restructured to consist of the following divisions: macroeconomic and manpower; sectoral and social planning; regional planning; projects development and review; and the technical assistance unit. The regional planning division was headed by an economist. The division also contained a range of skills including spatial planners. Papers were prepared on the importance of regional planning in a Jamaican context but these had little impact for several reasons some of which were outlined in Chapter II. Other reasons included the lack of cooperation and the fear of overlapping functions with other organisations. There was also some indecision about the focus of the division and whether it should be concerned with the problems of rural areas only as the lagging region or emphasis should be given to the preparation of regional plans. The division therefore did not have a smooth start and shortly after its establishment it began to lose staff.

Considerable effort was exercised, however, to prevent duplicity of activity with the Town Planning Department. Because of this fear there was a good deal of collaborative effort and a number of studies were jointly produced by both organisations. Most notably was the preparation of the 1978 to 1998 National Physical Plan which had a staff member of the National Planning Agency's regional planning division seconded to the Town and Country Planning Department to assist in the preparation of the plan. The cooperation between the agencies overall was good with the exception of the preparation of separate planning studies for the Kingston Metropolitan Region by both organisations.

The lack of a statement of clear vision on the role of regional planning in a national context ultimately led to the collapse of the regional planning division. In 1978, the division was merged with that of social planning to form a regional and social planning division. In 1984 the role of the National Planning Agency was expanded in a reorganised Planning Institute of Jamaica. The main functions of the PIOJ do include regional planning as was stated inter alia by the organisation in its Mission Statement in 1995:

> ...coordinating national, regional and sectoral development planning in order to facilitate the consistent and efficient implementation of projects and programs;

> PIOJ *40th Anniversary Supplement, 1995*

Despite this recognition of regional planning by the PIOJ there is not a separate division for regional planning. Thus regional planning has declined in importance from the position it held in the 1970s.

Bureau of Regional Affairs

In 1972 when the new administration outlined its national planning framework one important component was that of consultation. Not only was consultation to take place at the level of the consultative committees, but consultation was to take place with the general population. The Bureau of Regional Affairs was established primarily to facilitate consultation at a regional level

(Bonnick, 1995). Headed by a minister of state in the prime minister's office, the bureau had a small staff which was responsible for receiving letters from the public and identifying and implementing, on a pilot basis, local projects aimed at satisfying basic human needs. Once the project proved feasible it was transferred to the ministry responsible for that portfolio issue. One of the most successful projects undertaken by the bureau was that for 'special food shops'. This involved the establishment of shops that would sell food from the Agricultural Marketing Corporation at reduced prices in depressed communities in Kingston. Twenty such shops were to be established in a pilot project which included identifying the areas where the shops would be located, renting premises and hiring operators for the shops.

However, before the pilot project got off the ground the bureau was disbanded and most of its staff were transferred to the regional planning division of the NPA. This division therefore became involved in identifying locations and operators for the shops and ensuring that food in the Agricultural Marketing Corporation store was distributed and not left to spoil. The pilot project was such a great success that it was decided to extend the project to sixty shops island-wide and establish some special food truck routes (Bonnick, 1995). The expanded project was not as successful and like the bureau the entire project was soon disbanded. The collapse of the project was as a result of many factors coming together and having a negative impact. These factors included the lack of funds, the closure of the bureau and the transfer of the staff but not necessarily the vision and functions of the bureau itself.

The Regional Problem

SETTLEMENT GROWTH TRENDS

Jamaica's Settlement System
Jamaica's settlement system has evolved in response to a number of complex factors including the economic and cultural history of the country before 1940, location of good agricultural land, land ownership patterns, topographic features and more recently, the

development of the bauxite industry, manufacturing and tourism. The topography of the country largely encouraged initial concentration of development along the coast because the island's interior of relatively unproductive mountains was inhibitory to early settlement. The presence of a coastal fringe of fertile accessible plains complemented by numerous bays suitable for port development was the major factor that stimulated urban settlement along or near the shoreline. Several of the larger coastal towns became parish capitals because of their existing importance as market towns, communication centres and ports. This administrative function gave further impetus to growth. As the interior road system was established and the valleys were agriculturally developed, inland market towns grew, but these were much fewer and smaller than the coastal towns. Linstead, Bog Walk and Ewarton were all settled in the fertile St Thomas-in-the-Vale on the major north–south island road. May Pen developed along the banks of the Rio Minho on the main east–west road through southern Jamaica. May Pen's natural location advantage as a commercial centre for the sugar industry of Vere and for the transfer of goods by road and rail enhanced its importance as a major town. The growth of May Pen led to the Clarendon parish capital being relocated from Chapelton to May Pen.

The urban pattern reflects a traditional orientation of the economy to agriculture and port activities. The main urban centres are therefore located on the coast and in the midst of large agricultural areas. As we saw in Chapter IV the country is characterised by a poor development of its urban hierarchy which is illustrated in a city size distribution comprising one large city which dominates the network, few intermediate towns and a relatively large number of small towns. The colonial pattern of centralised administration also served to reinforce the pattern, and so, with the exception of the flourishing market towns of Mandeville, May Pen and Spanish Town the most important ports have come to serve as the administrative capitals for parishes.

Recent Economic Influences on the Growth of Towns and Cities
Within the last forty years the traditional economies of the urban

places, port activities and commercial and administrative centres serving the agricultural hinterland, have been supplemented and strongly influenced by the development of tourism, bauxite and manufacturing industries. The result is that sectoral changes in the economy translate directly into markedly uneven rates of regional settlement growth. In addition, changes in the economy at different periods of time also affect the country's spatial patterns and, in particular, urbanisation (Table VI).

Table VI: *Urban/Rural Population Change by Parish and Intercensal Periods*

Parish	% change 1960–1970		% change 1970–1982		% change 1982–1991		Annual rate of growth 1970–1991	
	Urban	Rural	Urban	Rural	Urban	Rural	Urban	Rural
Kingston	-9.30	–	-7.00	–	-6.30	–	-0.70	–
St Andrew	43.70	15.80	16.20	20.90	5.00	10.80	0.90	1.50
St Thomas	62.00	-8.60	15.90	8.90	4.30	4.00	1.90	0.60
Portland	29.80	-0.30	9.10	7.50	-1.90	3.60	0.60	0.40
St Mary	46.70	-1.00	7.70	3.70	-3.00	2.80	0.90	0.30
St Ann	53.80	-2.40	14.80	13.70	38.50	-0.60	2.40	0.60
Trelawny	45.20	4.00	14.80	7.50	2.40	-2.00	2.60	0.40
St James	85.30	-4.40	35.20	17.20	16.60	1.40	3.00	0.80
Hanover	29.70	7.00	7.80	4.20	-3.60	4.90	2.20	0.40
Westmoreland	69.40	-3.60	6.90	3.00	15.70	2.20	2.00	0.30
St Elizabeth	14.90	7.00	9.30	4.60	18.70	4.50	4.20	0.40
Manchester	64.90	0.30	18.60	0.20	8.60	8.90	3.40	0.40

Parish	% change 1960–1970		% change 1970–1982		% change 1982–1991		Annual rate of growth 1970–1991	
	Urban	Rural	Urban	Rural	Urban	Rural	Urban	Rural
Clarendon	54.50	-2.80	16.90	8.30	12.60	0.80	2.40	0.40
St Catherine	117.3	-5.60	84.40	5.20	23.60	-10.50	6.90	-0.30
Jamaica	38.90	-0.60	20.80	7.40	9.80	1.90	2.10	0.40

Source: 1960, 1970, 1982 and 1991 population censuses, STATIN

The 1991 population census of Jamaica estimated the population of the country at 2,366,067 (Statistical Institute of Jamaica, 1995). This represents an average annual intercensal growth rate of 0.86%, the lowest since 1943. The relatively low rate of increase between 1982 and 1991 has been due to net inflow of population rather than to any significant decline in the natural increase. The crude rate of natural increase which was 19.7 per thousand in 1982 declined to 19.2 in 1991. At the same time, the net outflow of population increased by 5.5% and thus reduced the increment to population by more than 50%. Indeed, based on information provided by the Statistical Institute's Demographic Statistics (STATIN, 1995) for the period between 1982 and 1991, net outflow reduced the natural increase of population by 57.4%.

More than one third of the population live in St Andrew and St Catherine. Just over one fifth, 22.8% of the population is located in St Andrew while 15.3% reside in St Catherine. Of the remaining parishes, Clarendon, Manchester and St James are the most populous with 9%, 6.9% and 6.6% of the population respectively. Over the period of 1982 to 1991, the parishes registering the highest percentage growth have been St James (14.85%), Manchester (14.55%), St Andrew (11.8%) and St Catherine (8.68%). Kingston declined by 0.25% (STATIN, 1995). Of particular significance since 1982 is the growth of the parish of St James. In 1970, approximately 5.5% of the total population of Jamaica lived in the parish of St James. By 1982 this proportion had increased to 6.2% and in 1991 it was 6.6%. The overall percentage increase since 1982 is 15%, representing an annual rate of growth of 1.6% (STATIN, 1995).

The position of Manchester should be noted also. This parish now contains 6.9% of the population compared with 6.6% in 1982 and shows an annual growth rate of 1.5% in the period of 1982 to 1991. St Andrew has continued to maintain its position as the parish with the largest portion of the population. It should be noted, however, that after the decline shown in this proportion in 1982, there has been an increase of 0.8% from 22% in 1982 to 22.8% in 1991. The rate of growth between 1982 and 1991 was 1.25% compared to 0.96% between 1970 and 1982. The parish showing the lowest rate of growth since 1982 is St Mary with a minimal 0.2% (STATIN, 1995).

The decline in the proportion of the population resident in Kingston, evident since 1960, has continued but with a slowing down in the rate of decline from 0.98% between 1970 and 1982 to 0.03% in the latest intercensal period (1982 to 1991). An examination of the growth rates over the thirty years since 1960 shows that it is the parish of St Catherine which has experienced the highest rate of growth, 2.8%, followed by St James, 2.06%. St Andrew and Manchester are the only other parishes exceeding the national total of 1.25%, with 1.96% and 1.26% respectively (STATIN, 1995). The spectacular growth of St Catherine's urban population has been due in large measure to the development of Portmore which grew by approximately 95% between 1970 and 1991 at an annual rate of growth of 20% as we saw in Chapter IV. The increasing importance of Montego Bay as a secondary city in the western part of the island accounts for the growth of the parish of St James.

Population distribution within the parishes since 1970 reflects a number of important shifts since that time. By far the most striking change has been the growth of St Catherine occurring simultaneously with a declining growth in the parish of Kingston (-0.76%). This is a reflection of new household formation in Kingston moving to the new suburbs and satellites located in St Catherine. The highest rates of growth for the entire period from 1970 to 1991 are seen in St Catherine, 3.6% and St James, 2%. Manchester, 1.25% is the only other parish with a rate which is higher than that of Jamaica at 1.3% (STATIN, 1995).

In terms of urban and rural distribution, apart from Kingston all of which is designated urban, St Andrew and St Catherine have the highest proportion of urban areas: 86% and 70% respectively. St Elizabeth with 90% of its population classified as rural is the parish with the highest proportion of rural population. In terms of urban growth between 1970 and 1991, the urban population of St Catherine exhibits the highest rate, 7%, followed by St Elizabeth, 4.2%, and Manchester, 3.4%. Only Portland, 0.6%, and St Mary, 0.9% showed growth of less than 1%. For the majority of the parishes, the rate of urbanisation was greatest during the intercensal period of 1960 to 1970; the exceptions were St Catherine,

St Elizabeth, Manchester, Trelawny and Hanover. Movement in the growth rates of the rural population show St Andrew to be the parish with the highest rate among this group, 1.5%, and St Catherine as the only parish with a declining rate of growth, -0.3%. All other parishes show a minimal rate of growth (STATIN, 1995).

The agricultural sector has suffered notable declines since the early 1960s when it accounted for 15% to 17% of GDP. The sector's contribution to GDP, expressed in constant prices, grew by J $30.9 million between 1973 and 1978. Since then there has been a declining trend so that by 1980 its share of GDP had fallen to 8.3%. While the measures introduced under the structural adjustment programme (deregulation of domestic and export marketing, improved farm gate pricing formulae for some export crops and improvements in credit level) contributed to improving incentives for farmers, they did not result in improved performance until the latter years of the 1980s. Banana production which had suffered persistent declines since the 1960s, rebounded strongly from 12,000 tonnes in 1985 to 41,628 tonnes in 1989 and 85,303 tonnes in 1995.

Sugar output which peaked in 1965 at 506,000 tonnes has been in decline ever since and despite efforts to improve performance, production was 207,000 tonnes in 1995. The agricultural sector's response in the first half of the 1980s to adjustment measures was disappointing, particularly in regard to export crop production and only since 1988 has there been some recovery which continued into the 1990s. As indicated in Table VII, there was some increase in employment in the agricultural parishes (Portland, St Mary) between 1982 and 1991, but this growth paled in comparison to increases in the parishes where tourism was the lead sector (St James, St Ann, Westmoreland and Hanover).

The performance of the bauxite and alumina industry depends on a number of factors, many of which are related to the global economic environment and the international demand for aluminium. During the 1970s, bauxite was the leading foreign exchange earner of the country. The growth in the bauxite industry attracted investment which led to the growth of resource-based towns and was responsible for the high rates of urbanisation in St Elizabeth and Manchester in the period between 1970 and 1982 when compared to the period between 1960 and 1970. The percentage increase of urban population between 1960 and 1970 was 14.9% in St Elizabeth and 64.9% in Manchester, compared with 101.1% and 85.6% respectively in the 1970 to 1982 intercensal period (see Table VI).

Between 1981 and 1985, owing to a major downturn in the international aluminium industry, total bauxite exports fell from 11.6 million tonnes to 6.2 million tonnes, a decline of 46% and bauxite and alumina contribution to GDP declined from 8.9% to 5.2%. With the increasing alumina prices in the latter part of the decade there was a reversal of this trend, with steady improvements in production and exports. An important contributor was the reopening of the Jamaica Aluminium Company (JAMALCO) smelter in Clarendon. The mining sector which had declined from 8.9% of GDP in 1980 to 5.2% in 1985 improved to 8.8% in 1993. Thus the sector which lost jobs during the early 1980s recovered sufficiently to provide employment in the bauxite parishes of Clarendon, Manchester and St Elizabeth in the intercensal period of 1982 to 1991.

During the 1980s, tourism emerged as the new leader among all the major economic sectors and since 1985 it has become the largest foreign exchange earner in the Jamaican economy. All major indicators of the sector show positive movements. In 1995, visitor arrivals totalled 1.7 million, gross visitor expenditure was US $965 million, hotel room occupancy rate was 60.8% and directly accounted for an estimated 31,154 full time jobs in 1995. This latter factor together with the indirect employment generated by the sector had a far reaching effect on urbanisation trends during the intercensal period of 1982 to 1991. As shown in Table VI the rate of urbanisation in the parish of St Ann in the intercensal period of 1982 to 1991 was at a much higher rate than the previous intercensal period and the rate of urban change exceeded all other parishes including St Catherine. This recent growth in the sector comes after early growth in accommodation that began in the late 1960s and allowed tourist arrivals to continue to expand into the mid-1970s. However, as a result of the downturn in demand in the mid-1970s after a period of hotel expansion, occupancy levels fell rapidly and many hotels experienced financial difficulties.

With high protection for import substitution, the manufacturing sector's performance had been stagnant throughout the 1970s and unreasonably high consumer prices, wasteful use of raw materials, and other inefficiencies were characteristic. Economic reforms of the 1980s resulted in an overall annual employment growth rate of 7.5% between 1982 and 1988 mainly as a result of job creation in the apparel sector. During the 1980s policy directives were focused on the transformation of the manufacturing sector from a predominantly import-substitution growth model to an export-propelled one, under the structural adjustment programme. Notwithstanding the efforts at adjustment and the emphasis on the development of non-traditional exports to third country markets, the sector's contribution to GDP in constant terms still remains below the levels obtained in the 1970s. As a whole, manufacturing increased from 15.4% of GDP in 1982 to 20.9% in 1987 and fell to 18.5% in 1995.

The export of apparel is the main variable affecting the overall value of manufactured exports. When the Free Zone exports are added, the total value of exports in 1991 totalled US $184.8 million and US $317 million in 1995. Within the last few years, however, garment production has run into troubled times and there have been factory closures as the industry has been affected by the North American Free Trade Agreement. Economic constraints such as high interest rates and the increasing cost of investment in manufacturing have had a negative impact on the sector in the 1990s and the growth in the apparel sub-sector was not sufficient to offset the decline in the other sub-sectors. Consequently, over the period between 1989 and 1993, employment in the manufacturing sector declined on average by 9,700 jobs annually and the percentage of the labour force employed in the sector fell from 15.2% in 1989 to 10.8% in 1995.

The economic climate and the policies pursued during the period of 1970 to 1991 resulted in the decline in the importance of the traditional activities, particularly agriculture, and an increase in the importance of tourism and manufacturing.

Between 1972 and 1982 an average of 7,200 jobs were created annually in the agriculture and mining sectors combined. However, the performance of the goods producing sector (agriculture, mining, manufacturing and construction) was disappointing in the 1980s, a trend which continued into the 1990s. The combined share of total employment in the sector declined from 50.8% in 1988 to 42.5% in 1993.

Location of employment is probably the most important single factor in urban growth. The data presented in Table VII provides some indication of how the parishes were affected by employment growth during the period between 1970 and 1991. Between 1970 and 1982 there was only a 3.4% increase in jobs compared with a 39.7% change between 1982 and 1991. St Catherine, Kingston and St James registered the greatest growth in employment between 1970 and 1982. It would appear therefore that during the 1970s, the manufacturing sector which predominates in the Kingston region (Kingston, St Andrew and St Catherine) dominated growth, followed by tourism, while the agricultural sector suffered declines as demonstrated in the loss of jobs in the parishes of Portland, St Mary, Hanover and St Catherine.

Possibly, as a consequence of the decline in employment opportunities, fewer persons have been seeking employment in these sectors, thereby creating a situation in which a decline in the labour force has exceeded increases in employment. However, employment in agriculture which has been declining since 1985 fell by 10.7% between 1992 and 1993. The reduction in the sector's employment share from 27.3% in 1992 to 24.4%, is significant, as for the first time, agriculture has lost its place as the single largest employer of labour.

Jobs in the service-producing sector suffered over the recession but have recovered robustly to compensate for any losses over the period. An average of 22,000 jobs were created in 1993, bringing the employment level to 507,900 in that year. This has brought about a significant shift in the sectoral composition of employment with the service-producing sector accounting for 56% of the employed labour force. Employment creation was concentrated primarily in hotels and restaurant services, with the employment level in the visitor accommodation sub-sector estimated at 31,154 persons in 1995. The Organisation of American States (OAS) Economic Impact Study found that the total number of persons directly employed in tourism was 2.8 times the amount employed in the accommodation sub-sector. If this ratio was the same in 1995, then estimates of the total number of persons directly employed in tourism would have amounted to 87,231. Direct employment in tourism accommodation increased from 9,585 in 1972 to 10,740 in 1976 and then fell to 8,482 with the decline of the sector in the mid-1970s. Between 1985 and 1995 direct employment in the sector has increased by 128.8% with employment in Ocho Rios increasing by 150% from 4,251 direct jobs in 1985 to 10,634 direct jobs in 1995. It should be noted, however, that the spectacular growth in employment in tourism has been in the period between 1991 and 1995. For example, between 1985 and 1989 direct employment in the sector in Port Antonio increased by 2.5% but actually doubled between 1991 and 1995.

Table VII: *Employment Change in Jamaica by Parish 1970–91*

Parish	Employed 1970	Employed 1980	Employed 1991	Absolute change		Percentage change	
				1970–1982	1982–1991	1970–1982	1982–1991
St Thomas	18,134	18,040	22,347	-94	4,307	-0.5	23.8
Portland	17,175	16,005	19,113	-1170	3,108	-6.8	19.4
St Mary	25,300	21,562	26,625	-3738	7,063	-14.7	32.7
St Ann	27,904	30,018	42,938	2,114	12,920	7.5	43.0
Trelawny	15,655	15,427	20,004	-228	4,577	-1.4	29.6
St James	28,101	32,673	47,483	4,572	14,810	16.2	45.3
Hanover	14,145	13,301	18,772	-844	5,471	-5.9	41.1
Westmoreland	26,018	25,825	34,769	-193	8,943	-0.7	34.6
St Elizabeth	28,508	29,350	38,814	842	9,464	2.9	32.2
Manchester	29,241	33,218	42,755	3,977	9,537	13.6	28.7
Clarendon	41,371	40,595	51,297	776	10,702	-2.6	26.3

Parish	Employed 1970	Employed 1980	Employed 1991	Absolute change			Percentage change	
				1970–1982	1982–1991		1970–1982	1982–1991
St Catherine	44,099	73,751	113,788	29,652	40,037		67.2	54.2
Kingston	33,343	23,881	30,165	-9,462	6,275		28.3	26.2
St Andrew	129,023	130,513	179,602	1,492	49,089		1.2	37.6
Total	478,017	494,159	690,463	16,142	196,304		3.4	39.7

Source: 1970, 1982, 1991 Population Censuses, STATIN

Settlement Growth

As indicated in Chapter IV the spatial system in Jamaica is characterised by the predominance of a primate city, a multiplicity of small rural central places and a growing but imperfectly developed middle base. In order to review the status and growth of urban places that make up the settlement system, all 134 urban places identified in the 1991 population census were grouped into six size classes as set out below (McHardy, 1997a). Urban places which cross parish boundaries were considered as one urban centre only.

Class VI Metropolitan KMA and Portmore
Class V   Large Over 15,000
Class IV Medium Large 10,001 – 15,000
Class III Medium 10,000 – 5,001
Class II Small 5,000 – 2000
Class I   Rural Centres Less than 2,000

Table VIII illustrates the decline in primacy of Kingston on the one hand and the growth of centres in the 'large' category since 1970. In that year slightly more than half of Jamaica's urban population lived in the KMA. By 1991, approximately 39.38% of the total urban population resided in the KMA or 46.24% if Portmore is included. In direct contrast was the growth of Class V centres. In 1970 there were three such centres with approximately 12% of the share of the urban population. By 1991 the number of centres had risen to six and the share of urban population to approximately 23%. The most impressive growth of these centres took place in the intercensal period between 1970 and 1982 when there was a 130% increase in population.

Table VIII: *Population Share of Urban Places in Jamaica 1970, 1982 and 1991*

Size class	Number of centres			Percentage of total urban population			Population change (%)	
	1970	1982	1991	1970	1982	1991	1970–82	1982–91
KMA	1	1	1	51.94	41.92	39.38	10.66	2.66
Portmore	1	1	1	0.24	6.21	6.86	3434.27	20.80
Class V	3	5	6	11.86	19.90	22.86	130.06	25.54
Class IV	3	2	3	3.92	2.18	2.80	-23.84	40.54
Class V	10	21	20	6.43	12.00	10.43	155.92	-4.98
Class II	47	55	61	14.91	12.50	13.30	14.95	16.25
Class I	69	49	42	10.71	5.29	4.38	-32.24	-9.66

Source: McHardy, 1997a, p.14

Table VIII also shows that the lowest order urban places are declining, with the greatest decline occurring between 1970 and 1982. The number of Class I places declined from 69 in 1970 to 42 in 1991, along with a decrease in their share of the urban population from 10.71% to 4.38%. However, this decline is as a result of the 'size-class jumping' phenomenon (Richardson, 1982). Most of these centres have actually grown and simply moved on to a higher class of urban places. The phenomenon of fast growth towns graduating to a higher urban category has to be considered. Banerjee and Schenk (1984) argue that the use of migration data may be one way of determining the performance of Class I urban places. This argument rests on the assumption that migration towards the larger urban places is predominantly caused by an overall low level of living conditions in rural areas, rural unemployment and a lack of off-farm employment opportunities in the nearby towns. Consequently, it can be maintained that if lower order centres were successfully performing their attributed functions their success should be clearly reflected in a reduced share of migrants to the larger centres (Banerjee and Schenk, 1984).

Unfortunately, it is not possible to determine from census data the share of urban population growth due to net rural to urban migration and if this share has been declining over the last three decades. Table IX, which indicates the proportion of urban places which have been growing and declining, tends to support the view of urban to urban migration contributing to the significant concentration of the population in the larger urban centres.

Table IX: *Population Growth and Decline by Size of Place, 1970–1982 and 1982–1991*

Population size of urban place	1970–1982		1982–1991	
	Growing (%)	Declining (%)	Growing (%)	Declining (%)
less than 2,000	76.06	23.94	74.00	26.00
2,000–5,000	88.10	11.90	69.23	32.69
5,001–10,000	100.0	—	70.00	30.00
10,001–15,000	100.0	—	100.0	—
over 15,000	100.0	—	100.0	—
KMA	100.0		100.0	
Portmore	100.0		100.0	

Source: McHardy, 1997a, p.16

Between 1970 and 1982, approximately 23.9% of Class I centres and 11.9% of Class II centres were declining, all other higher classes of centres were growing. During the intercensal period between 1982 and 1991, the proportion of declining centres in Class I remained approximately the same, 26%. However, declining centres in Class II rose to 33.7%. In addition, some decline in centres in the category 5,000 to 10,000 took place for the first time. As stated before, without disaggregation of the data to show the role of migration in this growth it is not possible to state conclusively based on population shares, that lower order centres were not performing their role, or to indicate whether a proportionally smaller share of migrants contributed to the growth of larger centres either than to the growth of lower order centres. (McHardy, 1997a).

While there has been overall growth in Jamaican towns included in the National Settlement Strategy between 1970 and 1991, it is important to note that trends that occurred during the periods of 1970 to 1982 and 1982 to 1991. Between 1970 and 1982 and 1982 and 1991, all regional centres grew, however, the situation was quite different for all other urban places in the settlement strategy, particularly among the sub-regional group.

Between 1970 and 1982, a few (5.6%) sub-regional centres declined, but between 1982 and 1991, the proportion of sub-regional centres that declined increased to 44.4%. These centres were Buff Bay, Highgate, Port Maria, Moneague, Lucea, Black River, Christiana Spaldings and Lionel Town. While this decline has been small in most of these centres, with the exception of Buff Bay, it is a worrying trend as centres at a sub-regional level should not be losing population. As stated earlier, without disaggregation of the data it is not possible to determine whether these centres are losing population to the regional centres in urban to urban migration. This also raises the issue of whether 1970 to 1982 marked the period of migration to the sub-regional centres and 1982 to 1991 a period of movement to the larger centres. This also brings in to question the impact of the National Settlement Strategy.

Settlement Economic Base

In order to determine the effect of economic activity on the growth of urban centres, settlements in the country were classified for the purpose of analysis into six categories based on their economic base or function as follows:

Group 1   traditional economies plus manufacturing industry and tourism

Group 2   traditional economies plus manufacturing industries

Group 3   traditional economies plus manufacturing industries and bauxite

Group 4   traditional economies plus manufacturing industries, bauxite and tourism

Group 5   traditional economies plus bauxite

Group 6   traditional economies plus tourism

Table X indicates the larger towns and cities whose recent growth has been affected by manufacturing, tourism and bauxite activities. In assessing the growth of these centres it should be noted that the defined boundaries of these areas are changed from time to time by STATIN, based on their continuous field assessments. In some cases, rapid development in an enumeration district which adjoins an urban locality, results in that enumeration district, hitherto classified as rural, being included in the urban fence. In much the same way an enumeration district which was previously included as part of a Special Area is excluded because the expected development does not materialise over time. The term Special Area is used by STATIN to designate any community which, in a Jamaican context, is of special interest. There are two types of Special Areas; urban and rural. Urban Special Areas include the KMA, all parish capitals and all other urban centres in Jamaica with a population of 2,000 or more persons.

The fact that the area of some Special Areas contracted while others expanded also provides important information about those centres which are growing and those centres which are either stagnant or declining. Special Areas which contracted in 1991 when compared with 1982 include Port Maria, Highgate and Buff Bay. Table X sets out the population of these areas for both 1982 and 1991 within the newly adjusted boundaries for 1991.

Table X: *Population of Contracting Centres within the same Boundaries for 1982 and 1991*

Centre	1982 (within 1991 boundaries)	1991 (within 1991 boundaries)	Annual rate of growth 1982–1991
Port Maria	6,646	7,196	0.89
Highgate	4,776	5,418	1.41
Christiana	6,437	7,235	1.31
Chapleton	3,456	3,930	0.61

Source: 1991 population census, STATIN

While the recalculation of the population as set out above would result in an increase in population between 1982 and 1991 rather than a decline, the important point is that in the intercensal period when Port Maria, Highgate, Christiana and Chapleton were contracting, other centres such as Ocho Rios and St Ann's Bay were growing as service centres and expanding in area.

Referring to Table XI, if Portmore is excluded, the urban places having the highest rates of growth between 1970 and 1991 were the regional centre of Mandeville (5.23%), the sub-regional centres of Negril (6.10%), Spanish Town (5.05%), Old Harbour (6.13%) and Morant Bay (5.0%), and the district centres of Runaway Bay (8.03%) and Whitehouse (8.25%). The Spanish Town–Old Harbour Area and Morant Bay may be considered as outlying areas of the KMA both in terms of residential development and receiving 'overspill industries', but the other centres have independent economic bases and each centre should be evaluated from this perspective.

Group 1 Centres

These centres are located on the north coast. All the centres except Oracabessa are parish capitals. In this group only Port Maria and Port Antonio grew at less than 2% per annum over the period of 1970 to 1991. Located in St Mary and Portland respectively, both centres are sited just outside of the north coast tourist belt and are market centres for the region's agricultural produce. This accounts for the slow growth of these centres between 1970 and 1991. Montego Bay and Falmouth gained substantially from tourism, although Montego Bay also gained from the expansion of industrial activity in the Montego Bay Free Zone. Montego Bay and Falmouth doubled their populations in the twenty years between 1970 and 1991.

Lucea's population increased at a rate of 2% annually between 1970 and 1991. However, the population of Lucea fell between 1982 and 1991 by 4%. Lucea like Port Maria and Port Antonio is more dependent on its agricultural and administrative functions to fuel growth. Like Port Antonio it has not gained substantially from the tourism boom on the north coast, hence its decline between 1982 and 1991. A J $6.5 million factory building programme by the Jamaica Industrial Development Corporation in Black River, Falmouth, Lucea and Savanna-la-mar largely accounts for the growth of these centres between 1970 and 1982.

Table XI: *Urban Population Change 1970–1991 by Size and Economic Function of the Urban Centre*

Urban centre	Classification	1970 population	1982 population	1991 population	Annual rate of growth 1970–91	Economic function
KMA	Metropolitan	473,700	524,200	538,144	0.6	1
Portmore	Metropolitan	2,197	77,448	93,799	19.6	–
Montego Bay	Regional centre	43,521	70,265	82,002	3.1	1
Port Antonio	Regional centre	10,426	12,285	13,118	1.1	1
Falmouth	Sub-regional centre	3,855	6,713	7,955	3.5	1
Port Maria	Sub-regional centre	5,441	7,508	7,196	1.3	1
Lucea	Sub-regional centre	3,579	5,652	5,419	2.0	1
Oracabessa	District centre	2,216	4,189	4,066	2.9	1
Spanish Town	Sub-regional centre	39,204	87,975	110,379	5.1	2
May Pen	Regional centre	25,425	40,962	45,903	2.9	2

Table XI (continued): *Urban Population Change 1970–1991 by Size and Economic Function of the Urban Centre*

Urban centre	Classification	1970 population	1982 population	1991 population	Annual rate of growth 1970–91	Economic function
Old Harbour	Sub-regional	5,097	15,107	17,778	6.1	2
Savanna-la-mar	Sub-regional centre	11,604	14,912	16,340	1.6	2
Linstead	Sub-regional centre	5,996	9,205	14,144	4.2	2
St Ann's Bay	Regional centre	7,101	9,058	10,961	2.1	2
Morant Bay	Sub-regional centre	3,482	8,823	9,602	5.0	2
Christiana	Sub-regional centre	7,344	8,894	7,235	-0.1	2
Brown's Town	Sub-regional centre	5,479	6,351	6,762	1.0	2
Highgate	Sub-regional centre	5,636	5,975	5,418	-0.2	2

Table XI (continued): *Urban Population Change 1970–1991 by Size and Economic Function of the Urban Centre*

Urban centre	Classification	1970 population	1982 population	1991 population	Annual rate of growth 1970–91	Economic function
Lionel Town	Sub-regional centre	3,362	4,739	4,669	1.7	2
Chapleton	District Centre	4,163	5,304	3,390	-0.3	2
Black River	Sub-regional centre	2,701	3,601	3,590	1.4	2
Mandeville	Regional centre	13,681	34,502	39,945	5.2	4
Ocho Rios	Regional centre	5,851	7,777	8,189	1.6	4
Santa Cruz	Sub-regional centre	2,050	5,979	8,144	6.8	5
Hayes	Sub-regional centre	4,258	6,457	8,447	3.3	5
Runaway Bay	District centre	1,116	2,838	5,655	8.0	6

Table XI (continued): *Urban Population Change 1970–1991 by Size and Economic Function of the Urban Centre*

Urban centre	Classification	1970 population	1982 population	1991 population	Annual rate of growth 1970–91	Economic function
Negril	Sub-regional centre	1,311	2,570	4,184	6.1	6
Whitehouse	District centre	598	515	3,157	8.3	6

Sources: 1970, 1982 and 1991 population censuses, STATIN

Oracabessa which grew by 2.9% annually between 1970 and 1991, actually declined by 2.9% between 1982 and 1991 after experiencing an increase in population of 89% between 1970 and 1982. With the closure of the banana port in 1970, there was a proposed tourism development by the Urban Development Corporation which did not materialise as envisaged, but a large number of subdivisions, some premature, took place in the Oracabessa area.

Group 2 Centres

Except for Morant Bay, Black River, Savanna-la-mar, St Ann's Bay and Old Harbour–Old Harbour Bay all the towns and cities in Group 2 are inland towns serving agricultural hinterlands. As stated earlier, the growth of Spanish Town, Old Harbour and Morant Bay is closely linked to the growth of the KMA. Old Harbour's growth has also been influenced by the export of alumina from Port Esquivel.

May Pen and Lionel Town are located on the southern plains of Clarendon. The area is devoted to sugar cane cultivation and sugar is milled and refined in the Monymusk Factory which was recently upgraded under a World Bank programme. Some twenty years ago Alcoa set up an alumina production plant at Hayes which was closed in the late 1970s. It was reopened in 1985 as the more efficient Jamalco which led to the expansion of job opportunities in May Pen to service the industry. May Pen's growth between 1970 and 1991 was due to the expansion of agricultural service functions. Some diversification of manufacturing and service jobs related to the bauxite industry. Lionel Town's slower growth of only 1.7% compared to May Pen's growth of 2.9% is due to its dependency on the growing and manufacture of sugar.

Located on the major north-south island road, Linstead grew up as an inland market town in the fertile St-Thomas-in-the-Vale. Linstead's growth, like that of May Pen, has been indirectly influenced by the development of the bauxite industry, Jamaica's second refinery was built at Ewarton by Alcan in 1959. Recent growth in Linstead is as a result of expansion of agricultural service functions, some diversification into manufacturing and servicing the needs of the bauxite industry. The other inland towns of Christiana, Highgate, Chapleton and Browns Town

213

Figure 6.3: The traditional economies of urban places have been supplemented and strongly influenced by the development of tourism, bauxite and manufacturing industries.

remained stagnant or experienced some decline. Except for Brown's Town, these centres were not located close enough to either bauxite or tourism to feel the indirect effects and their dependency on the agriculture sector accounted for their stagnation.

St Ann's Bay, Savanna-la-mar and Black River are all parish capitals and have important administrative functions. Both St Ann's Bay and Savanna-la-mar have gained indirectly from the tourism industry. Savanna-la-mar has long been the centre of the sugar industry in the western part of the island. Approximately 45% of the country's total sugar production comes from this region and is processed in the island's largest sugar factory located there. However, with the growth of tourism in Negril, new businesses were set up in Savanna-la-mar to service the needs of the tourist infrastructure, and the population in the region's network of townships grew as employment opportunities increased.

St Ann's Bay is located at the centre of the north coast tourist belt and owes a large part of its growth to the expansion of the tourist industry along the section of the coast from Discovery Bay to Oracabessa. As the administrative capital and the market centre for the region's agricultural produce, its economic base has been strengthened and expanded as a result of the tourist industry. The success of tourist development along this coastal strip has injected a dynamic element into the region's economy as new businesses have been set up in St Ann's Bay to service the needs of the tourist sector. The town has also derived indirect benefits from the large number of persons employed in the tourist industry in Ocho Rios but who reside in St Ann's Bay where residential accommodation is easier to obtain.

Black River, like Lucea, (Group 1), presents an interesting scenario. During the twenty-year period the population of the town has grown by just more than 30% at an annual rate of 1.4%, but in the latest intercensal period, has remained almost static. Black River was the major port for log-wood and dye exporting the products of two log-wood factories in the parish. With the collapse of the dye industry Black River's importance died with the industry. Because of their aridity, the nearby Pedro Plains could not produce the traditional export crops further limiting the growth of the town.

Group 4 Centres

Mandeville and Ocho Rios make up the centres in Group 4 comprising traditional economies but benefiting also from the manufacturing industry, bauxite and tourism. Bauxite, tourism and manufacturing all have strong location factors. The bauxite industry has developed at or near bauxite deposits with port facilities constructed within reasonable distance from the mining areas and/or alumina plants. The bauxite industry employees have also tended to live in nearby existing towns. Mandeville is a notable example of a long-established town which has expanded very rapidly in recent years based on nearby bauxite and alumina operations. Mandeville has also been attracting a large number of returning residents in recent times. This trend, together with the improved performance of the bauxite industry and a growing service sector, have no doubt contributed to Mandeville's population increase between 1970 and 1991.

Until the mid-1980s, the economic base of Ocho Rios was the production of bauxite based on the operations of Reynolds Jamaica at Belmont in St Ann. Bauxite was shipped from port facilities at Ocho Rios which were shared with a fleet of small fishing vessels. While some private hotels were developed in Ocho Rios in the early 1980s, the centre of commercial and administrative activities was the town of St Ann's Bay. However, two major changes occurred in the mid-1980s which influenced growth in Ocho Rios. The general decline in the bauxite industry led to the closing of the Belmont production site and secondly, Ocho Rios became the location for a major tourist development programme, managed by the UDC. As a result of these changes, Ocho Rios was transformed into the centre of Jamaica's cruise ship industry, and a variety of tourist-related services began to locate there.

In terms of population growth, however, Ocho Rios has one of the lowest growth rates (1.6%) between 1970 and 1991 of all urban centres listed in Table IV. One of the reasons for this relates to the fact that growth in Ocho Rios has been tempered by its juxtaposition to St Ann's Bay which has important administrative functions and is an important market centre for the region's agricultural produce. St Ann's Bay has grown because the indirect benefits of the tourist industry have resulted in the expansion of its mix of services and catchment area. The other major factor which has contributed to this slower growth rate is the growth of major squatter settlements outside of the 1991 Special Area of Ocho Rios. Between 1970 and 1982 squatter settlements emerged within the Special Area at Green Bay and Buckfield. Between 1982 and 1991, squatter communities have sprung up outside the Special Area.

Group 5 Centres

These have grown as a result of their location at Hayes, or near Santa Cruz, bauxite deposits. Santa Cruz has grown up as a result of being located at the centre of the bauxite industry in St Elizabeth. In 1969, a plant was constructed at Nain in St Elizabeth by Alpart. In 1971, Revere Copper and Brass opened the island's fourth alumina plant at Maggotty in St Elizabeth. This latter plant has since closed, but Santa Cruz, because of its location, has gained importance as a thriving commercial and service node rather than the parish capital, Black River. As a result of its importance as a centre serving the bauxite industry there has been increased subdivision and residential activity in the area. Hayes is the centre of bauxite and alumina industry in Clarendon, but its growth has not been as spectacular as Santa Cruz because of the dominance of May Pen as a regional centre.

Group 6 Centres

These centres are those which owe their growth entirely to the development of the tourist industry. These centres have grown at a faster rate than those centres which had factors other than tourism contributing to their growth. These are also relatively small centres and in some cases lacked the absorptive capacity to cope with this growth. In Negril, for example, the growth of squatter settlements in the town is a major impact of its growth.

It is possible to conclude from analysis that the growth of towns has been related to the provision of employment opportunities. Towns which have experienced substantial expansion in employment over the last decade have experienced high rates of population increase. Growth in employment has been in tourism,

217

manufacturing and other services. Growth in the bauxite industry has had a significant impact on the centres which directly served the industry, but its effects have been felt to a lesser extent throughout the parish when compared to the tourist industry. Centres which depend on agriculture to generate rural job opportunities have suffered decline. As a result it is the secondary towns, with a population of over 15,000, which have grown. Smaller centres which serve the rural area and have an important role to play in functional development in these areas have been declining.

Role of Spatial Strategies in National Development

IMPACT OF ECONOMIC DEVELOPMENT ON THE SPATIAL STRUCTURE

As we have seen in the previous section the changing trends in Jamaica's settlement system are linked to structural shifts in the national economy. The result is that sectoral changes in the economy translate directly into markedly uneven rates of regional growth. For example, the growth in the bauxite industry has attracted investment and led to the growth of resource-based towns (e.g. Mandeville and Santa Cruz) and has been responsible for the high rate of urbanisation in St Elizabeth and Manchester during the intercensal period of 1970 to 1982.

Similarly, it has been noted that during the past thirty years the urban primary index has declined steadily. However, this change cannot be attributed to any explicit urbanisation or spatial policies as there are no urban policies directly intended to favour or discourage urban growth. Here the decline suggests that throughout the seventies and eighties the growth of the primary city, Kingston, experienced 'overspill' growth in Spanish Town and Portmore. Residential and industrial development in Spanish Town is linked to the economic base of Kingston.

Implementation of Regional Plans and Policies

Despite the preparation of the National Settlement Strategy and various regional plans, there was little official recognition of the strong linkage between the development of settlements and broad economic processes until the publication of the five year plan 1990–1995. This five-year redevelopment plan was the first to devote a separate chapter to the subject 'Urban and Rural Development'. It stressed the need for balanced urban, rural and regional development in order to ensure the optimal use of the country's limited resources and for the population to attain adequate living standards. The fundamental objective of the government in regard to this plan was to foster more spatial development by ensuring that the relative deficiencies in rural sectors are taken into account in future investment decision making. This objective was to be achieved through a number of strategies.

Despite these ambitious goals, the desired objective has not been achieved as the government's macroeconomic policies indirectly affect spatial patterns. Government programmes for investment and growth are directed at all sectors regardless of location. Because of the nature of actions included in these projects, investment is normally spread throughout the country according to sector priorities set up by the different agencies in charge of their implementation. Thus investment decisions made by the government are made at a macroeconomic level indicating that no explicit spatial development policy is currently giving guidance to decision making in this respect. The result is that macroeconomic policies have been influencing spatial patterns in an indirect way and often with unintended biases.

Comprehensive Rural Township Development

Perhaps the only real attempt at implementing some kind of regional planning scheme has been the Comprehensive Rural Township Development Programme (CRTDP) which is being undertaken by the Urban Development Corporation. The CRTDP was formulated as the means through which the Urban Structure and Policy would be implemented. The approach was to identify the focal point and sphere of influence of what would be considered the region which the project would impact. The original programme was designed to improve the quality of small town and rural life through the development of regions which had the potential for agriculture development or a solid economic base, by providing the necessary basic infrastructure and helping to improve the quality of life. In 1983, the government of Jamaica received a loan from the Inter-American Development Bank for the implementation of Phase I of the programme. The total loan programme was to the amount of US $22 million, with the IDB providing approximately 75% and the government 25%. Construction activities of Phase I began in July 1985 and a completion date was scheduled for July 1986. A second phase of the programme commenced in 1987. However, as a result of damages inflicted by Hurricane Gilbert in 1988, the IDB and the government agreed to reformulate the programme in order to make uncommitted resources available for funding works of restoration and repair of rural roads, health facilities and schools.

An important consideration of the CRTDP is that it is planned and implemented as a programme of the UDC. It is quite possible therefore, that towns selected by the UDC bear no relationship to the towns selected for development emphasis by any of the other development agencies. The point being that there is no sector integration of the various development agencies using the urban centre as the basic unit for integrated plan formulation, implementation and coordination.

The components of Phase I of the programme included the provision of educational skills, primary health care, community centres and the upgrading of access roads. The first objective of the educational component of the educational skills component of the programme was to provide educational opportunities in selected locations within the project regions in order to enable students leaving school to acquire basic organisational skills as required for employment or self-employment in the local economy. The second objective was to contribute to a reduction in unemployment among young people who leave the educational system without adequate training for work.

Vocational and secondary schools were constructed at three district centres (Cascade, Mavis Bank and Newmarket–Lewisville), and secondary schools were constructed at the sub-regional centre Christiana-Spaldings (considered as one centre in the National Settlement Strategy). In an ex-post evaluation of the project it was stated that, overall, the programme was successful because of the construction, furnishing and equipping of the social facilities which provided improved and more accessible services which, in turn, contributed to an improved quality of life for the targeted population. The majority of the facilities provided were used by the residents of the targeted communities and in some instances, by residents from areas much further afield than was originally intended (UDC, 1992).

Phase III of the CRTDP has been modified, based on the premise that the prosperity of small towns is increasingly dependent on their ability to provide qualified labour and services to secondary cities. Phase III will therefore continue to give priority investments in townships, but it will concentrate on those townships that serve 'micro regions' that are making the most contribution to Jamaica's balance of payments. Phase III has conceived each micro region in terms of an urban centre together with a hinterland to which it is functionally linked through the flows of goods and services. By doing this, CRTDP envisages that the regions will continue to be productive and attractive, without increasing the incentives to migrate to the urban centre. Phase III, by concentrating investments in a relatively limited number of regions, also envisages that the community will be more likely to perceive a significant improvement in the standard of living, while the services themselves will have important complementarities (UDC, 1991). Phase III which commenced in 1997 will be funded by the IDB.

Setting the Framework for Regional Planning

EVALUATING THE NATIONAL SETTLEMENT STRATEGY

The National Settlement Strategy has not had the desired results with regard to promoting the role of small and medium-sized towns in economic and spatial development, and reducing regional imbalances and as a consequence rural to urban migration. The explanation for this lies in the weak implementation of the strategy. The CRTDP cannot effect the necessary change and reduce regional disparities if there is no long-term commitment to the pursuit of spatial policies at broader national and sector levels. There are currently two major constraints associated with the implementation of the NSS, the role of local government in the process and the lack of integration between macroeconomic policies and spatial planning.

The Role of Local Government

Power and resources are highly centralised in Jamaica despite the current Local Government Reform Programme where efforts are being made to give more autonomy to the local authorities. Lack of power, personnel and resources at local levels of government means that small and intermediate settlements cannot act as the centres through which the needs and priorities of local populations and communities are articulated and passed to higher levels of government. In addition, poor access to several towns and the large parish areas which are served by the parish councils, reinforces the tendency for council members to focus on the main urban centres of the parish.

Until the advent of the Local Government Reform Programme little attempt had been made by central government to guarantee the parish councils the power and the skilled personnel to develop and collect their own revenue base. Increasingly local authorities must play a more important role in planning and investment coordination. The parish councils should therefore be provided with the resources and staff to ensure coordination between the public agencies and ministries working on sector projects within or affecting their area, and for the successful implementation of development plans.

The Role of Macroeconomic Policies and Sector Plans

Non-spatial policies and sector plans which have important spatial biases tend to diffuse the direct impact of spatial policies. Richardson (1982) points to the powerful spatial impacts of various macroeconomic policies, such as those which promote import substitution. Governmental support for the development of particular sectors has the effect of subsidising productive investments in the locations which best serve the new or expanding protected industrial activities. A large proportion of investment is spread throughout the country according to sector priorities set up by different agencies in charge of their implementation. These projects have a profound impact on spatial development, but none of these projects is guided by quantitative targets for growth in different locations. In addition, very few of the projects establish links between the sectors of the regional economy, thus reducing the possibilities of increasing regional capacity to achieve a greater degree of self-sustained regional development.

Updating the National Settlement Strategy

It would appear that in the selection of small and intermediate settlements there are a number of factors that must be considered. First, not every small or intermediate settlement has the potential for strategic economic growth in a national development context. At any one time, only a few small or intermediate settlements will be able to assume a strategic role in national development, and only those with promising prospects should be so designated (UNCHS, 1985). One of the failures of the NSS can be directly attributed to the dilution of impact because of the attempt to promote too many centres.

A second point of consideration is the limitations imposed by public investment resource constraints. Central government does not have available to it sufficient resources, personnel or finances to play all the development roles involved in creating and managing a NSS consisting of 101 centres. Choices will have to be made about which centres should receive investment funding. Available resources are currently limited relative to the investment needs of all the towns and cities as well as the full range of competing demands within the country; it is important therefore to apply these resources where they can be most productive.

It would appear therefore, that three important issues need to be addressed at this time: a conceptual framework for the implementation of the NSS; a selection of target towns and cities; and operational mechanisms for supporting urban growth. The position regarding the implementation of the NSS is that there is no framework within which it operates. There are 101 centres in the strategy and any centre can be selected at any time for any reason. This is not a rational or feasible approach to development and certainly not one the country can afford. There is therefore a need to devise a conceptual framework in which the strategy must operate.

An important starting point is to review the selection process used by the UDC for the Comprehensive Rural Township Programme in order to ensure that resources that are available are directed at achieving national development objectives. To recapitulate: the original programme was designed to improve the quality of small towns and rural life through the development of regions which had a potential for agricultural development or a solid economic base, by providing the necessary basic infrastructure and services required by the community in each region. It consisted of infrastructure works – roads, drainage, secondary schools and health centres – to be carried out in twenty townships. In the aftermath of Hurricane Gilbert the programme was redesigned to take care of urgent repairs. So in actual fact eleven centres were addressed over a period of seven years.

The current programme is designed to adapt the NSS to Jamaica's current macroeconomic circumstances. The general goal is to improve the quality of public services in the townships of Jamaica's most economically dynamic areas, particularly those contributing to the strengthening of Jamaica's balance of trade. The programme will therefore: set up and implement a procedure for identifying and selecting micro regions associated with centres of high economic growth; set up and implement a system for identifying and selecting priority investment projects in the townships of eligible regions; finance priority investments to improve the coverage and service quality provided by the townships' public infrastructure; and coordinate the activities of local support committees to promote the proper operation and maintenance of the constructed projects.

There are four alternative models of urban development: model of concentration; model of selective concentration; model of selective dispersal; and model of complete dispersal (Sharma, 1984). The model of concentration increases rural to urban migration, increases regional disparity and lays excessive strain on urban services. The model of selective concentration is based on the growth pole theory and allows for a relative predominance of the metropolitan centres while simultaneously developing productive activities in select strategically located small urban centres. The selective dispersal model with its hierarchical arrangement of settlements and the distribution of services therein, is rural development oriented. Complete dispersal provides for a high degree of distribution of employment and services but requires a high financial input and strong planning and implementing machinery (Sharma, 1984).

Phase I of CRTDP followed to some extent the selective dispersal model, particularly where an attempt was made to link type I and type II health centres in the south Clarendon health district. On the other hand, Phase III of CRTDP has opted for a model of concentration. While CRTDP III lays emphasis on the importance of the micro region, it is the main towns in the region that are receiving the most attention. Roads which provide access to small rural communities and link agricultural production areas with market towns in the said region are considered as part of the programme, but the programme is designed to address the problems of the secondary towns. What is required therefore, is a complementary programme targeted at the small and intermediate settlements in the micro regions identified in CRTDP III. In other words the conceptual framework for implementation of the NSS should be one of selective concentration. Such a framework would allow CRTDP III to be linked with a cluster of intermediate towns in defined regions.

In order to proceed in this manner it will not be possible to address the entire hierarchy of towns and cities in the National Settlement Strategy all at once. Some formal selection process is necessary to identify promising candidates for special treatment among the national pool of 101 small and intermediate settlements. Since the promulgation of the NSS in 1970, Jamaica has only been to undertake work in eleven centres for a variety of reasons, of which lack of available resources is a major one. USAID (1985) in four case studies on secondary city development programmes found that no country, no matter how endowed with resources, is able to address the entire hierarchy of towns and cities in a single programme effort.

The potential envisaged in 1970 of some of the centres in the NSS has not materialised. Some communities need certain types of investment and assistance before they can be expected to support new enterprise or institutional structures for managing modern urban infrastructure. Within the resource constraints of

Jamaica a model of complete dispersal is neither feasible nor possible. The conceptual framework should form the context for the selection of centres for priority treatment. Every effort should be made to make maximum use of available resources by linking projects in the various towns. CRTDP III provides the basis for initiating a comprehensive, integrated development programme in other towns as well as those selected for CRTDP III.

The long range objective should be to attract industry and skilled and semi-skilled labour to CRTDP III towns and other secondary towns. However, these urban centres must be provided with some basic level of infrastructure and the necessary amenities before they can attract and support industrial operations. The strategy, therefore, calls for linking improvements in urban infrastructure with agricultural modernisation efforts, especially around the smaller urban centres. Such a programme should be approached in a selective manner, concentrating on those urban centres showing the best prospects for economic development and the greatest capacity to absorb funds in productive investments. The intention is to concentrate on four or five centres that make up an 'urban cluster'. Projects should be selected in these urban areas with a view to supporting existing, or establishing new, economic and social activities that can contribute to economic dynamism of the entire sub-region. Such an approach would involve the weeding out of those centres which have been declining in terms of population and employment and which lack services and leadership potential to be considered 'growth points'.

Other crucial issues facing the success of the NSS revolve around improving institutional coordination, creating stronger linkages between planning and implementation and strengthening urban and spatial planning and management. In this regard, project implementation requires a more explicit consideration of the socio-economic and spatial impacts of projects at the regional level throughout the whole project development and implementation process. With respect to integration there is need to integrate budgets and focus the investment of resources on the achievement of agreed targets. Projects are being proposed and designed by specific sector organisations and ministries of government. The multiplication of agencies implementing the same kind of projects prevents linkages between projects, both in overall terms (e.g., more flexible use of the total investment devoted by the country to a particular problem), and in specific circumstances.

Chapter VII

PLANNING IMPACTS: THE PAST, THE PRESENT AND THE FUTURE

In this final chapter we will examine the overall effects of spatial planning policies since the introduction of statutory town planning and we also look at some alternatives for the way forward. It should be noted, however, that very few studies have been undertaken on the impact of the various planning policies in Jamaica and it has therefore been very difficult to assess the overall impact of all the policies. As we saw in Chapter V planned decentralisation efforts were somewhat stymied because policy initiatives and instruments were not harmonised effectively. A similar type of assessment, as was done in 1965 in Great Britain and which produced the PAG report, has never been done in Jamaica.

The National Physical Plans of 1970 to 1990 and 1978 to 1998 established the National Settlement Strategy as the spatial framework to guide socio-economic development so that urbanisation would proceed on a rational basis. The underlying principle of the strategy is that urbanisation in itself is not an undesirable result of national development, but rather is a natural accompaniment to economic growth and if guided carefully, can become an important agent for social and economic progress. On this basis, it was determined that there was need for a clearly articulated urban policy, which would be implemented according to an urban structure and policy. However, the degree of coordination expected with reference to the National Settlement Strategy has not occurred. Settlement policies involve the integration of a number of different ministries and agencies. Each of these ministries and agencies view their responsibilities to settlement planning differently and are influenced by differences in substantive policy directives and resource constraints.

Planners have not played a major role in influencing the form and content of development programmes or in helping to ensure a more equitable distribution, in human and spatial terms, of development opportunities, and of the social and economic benefits which result from development. This has been due in large measure to the traditional forms of planning, administration and legislation which were taken over from former colonial administrations and, in a situation where financial and other resources are limited, these forms have little relevance. There is an urgent need to recognise the links between spatial strategies and economic and sectoral policy. Policies for economic development must recognise their locational implications and the role of the planner must be strengthened to develop an institutional framework that creates real coordination.

Assessment of Legal and Institutional Arrangements

LEGAL

It has long been recognised that the legal basis for planning in Jamaica needs to be reformed by incorporating the substance of the Local Improvements Act into an expanded Town and Country Planning Act. This would allow for one integrated system of development activities relating to land. As we saw in Chapter III the main impact of having two different authorities governing the land development process is a great waste of effort and cost being expended in a process which is not satisfactory. The process involves considerable unnecessary paperwork and agency time having to deal with subdivision and development as two different applications. As we also saw in Chapter III considerable effort has gone into reforming the mechanics of the process, but there is a need for changes to the Town and Country Planning Act.

Currently, a bill is being prepared to repeal the existing Town and Country Planning Act and to make new provisions related to town and country planning. This new Act will incorporate subdivisions as a development under the Act. A proposed revision entitled Third Revision of Bill was circulated in 1997 and was criticised on the grounds that it gave too much power to the minister in charge of planning. On the other hand the role of the local planning authority would be drastically diminished under the new Act. Questions were also raised about the role of the Town and Country Planning Authority in the preparation of development orders. Under the new Act the Town and Country Planning Authority would have the power to contract the preparation of development orders to private individuals and firms. While the Town Planning Department has suffered from a serious loss of staff since the 1980s and has problems of recruiting trained and competent staff, contracting out planning responsibilities would not create a sound professional planning capability for Jamaica. In addition such an approach would reinforce the physical and land use aspects of planning rather than reconditioning the process to reflect the policy basis of planning and new thinking which should address Jamaica's needs.

Planners in the country are concerned that the Town and Country Planning Act is being repealed and replaced by a new Act, without any real diagnostic study being conducted of what is best suited to Jamaica. Revamping the 1957 Town and Country Planning Act is viewed as not being particularly relevant at this time as the Act was drafted specifically for the purposes of development control. There is a strong feeling among planners in the country that the process of amending the Act needs to be more inclusionary and that more professional planners should be involved in the process. There is also a need to review all laws and institutional arrangements involved in the land development process to ensure that conflicts and overlaps are resolved, and above all the new Act must be cognisant of the needs and realities of planning in Jamaica. The Act should not be seen as the means through which power is exercised but rather the mechanism to ensure that the planning process is facilitated.

INSTITUTIONAL

As we saw in Chapter III several institutional initiatives have been undertaken to improve the approval process. By the middle of the year 2001 the Town Planning Department will be replaced by a

National Environmental Planning Agency (NEPA). This new agency will be formed by joining the Town Planning Department with the Natural Resources Conservation Authority. It is expected that once NEPA comes into force the processing time required for approval of development applications will be considerably reduced as a 'one-stop' service institution will be established.

However, providing a sound professional planning capability for Jamaica is much more than ensuring the timely processing of development applications. A more integrated outlook on all development efforts taking place in a parish or region is necessary at this time. Policies to support the developmental roles that small and intermediate settlements can play, needs coordinated action between sector ministries and local government. Cross-sectoral, region-wide strategies are required to minimise any unnecessary duplication of initiatives and to ensure the coordination of land use and other activities that are fundamental to achieving a balance between environmental, economic and social objectives of sustainable development. In this regard, more emphasis should be placed on developing and monitoring long-term strategies that satisfy the broader goals of regional development.

Spatial Impacts of Planning

URBAN RENEWAL

The earliest urban renewal programmes involved re-housing in the older parts of Kingston. Redevelopment mainly took the form of tenements and terraced housing. However, some of these programmes still represent some of the worst forms of housing found in the city today. The first major urban renewal programme in the country was aimed at the CBD to combat decline and decentralisation. By 1960, major changes had taken place in the commercial activities of the city. As the built-up areas of the city expanded, the CBD was no longer at the centre of the city, but was in fact located at a peripheral position in relation to the new suburbs. In addition, the CBD was becoming increasingly congested, with several streets dating back to the seventeenth century and there was a lack of adequate planning.

Planning was intended to play a major role in rehabilitating the city core of Kingston and restoring the commercial functions of downtown Kingston. The Kingston Waterfront Redevelopment Company was established explicitly for this purpose and set about preparing a plan for the redevelopment of the waterfront. However, such efforts were thwarted by the economic difficulties facing the country beginning in the 1970s and by the suburbanisation taking place in the KMA about the same time. The UDC created under its own Act had few, if any, links with the existing planning machinery and as a result there was very little collaboration between the UDC and the Town Planning Department. The corporation was pursuing the development of the waterfront as an agency of government using mainly public sector sources for financing. The Town Planning Department on the other hand, was primarily concerned with monitoring the activities of private developers through the Town and Country Planning Act. Approvals were being given to private developers by the Town Planning Department for the development of alternate commercial nodes closer to the centre of population such as New Kingston.

These activities actually point to inconsistencies in the planning system whereby outlying commercial nodes have undermined the importance of the CBD as the main commercial and office centre. The development of alternate nodes to downtown Kingston still remains the most powerful inhibiting factor to the regeneration of downtown and will pose problems for the recently launched Tax Incentive Programme as in the current economic environment it will be difficult to support developments in New Kingston and downtown Kingston.

URBAN GROWTH

Suburban Development

Planning has had a major impact on urban growth, both planned and unplanned. Suburban growth in the KMA was set long before the advent of the Town and Country Planning Act. The growth of the KMA has taken the form of adding subdivisions to the city to meet the demand for houses according to the increase of the city's population. Growth of the city's population spread from Kingston to the adjoining parishes of St Thomas and St Catherine in a basically unplanned manner. Because of the increasing scarcity of large tracts of land for housing schemes there was the tendency for residential construction to shift out from the Liguanea Plain on which Kingston is situated. This trend began in the 1960s when a number of major subdivisions took place in St Thomas extending the city further eastwards. In the 1970s there was a further shift in emphasis from Kingston to St Catherine in the west where the Liguanea Plain grades into the St Catherine Plains and facilitates the growth of the city across the Rio Cobre in the direction of Spanish Town. The St Catherine Plains have traditionally been under extensive sugar cane cultivation or used as pasture land.

Most of these developments demonstrate the strong influence of planning in terms of design and guidelines set out in the development orders. However, the development orders guiding growth in the region, namely Spanish Town, St Catherine Coast and Kingston were prepared either in 1964 or 1965. They therefore do not provide guidance in terms of overall urbanisation patterns in the region, and the 1973 Kingston Regional Plan which made recommendations for urban development was never implemented. The result has been rapid urban growth in the region and demands for urban services and maintenance of basic utilities have outstripped the capacity of both local and central government to provide them. There is also strong competition for surface and groundwater supplies between urban and agricultural areas. Neither the domestic nor the irrigation needs of the region are being adequately met by current water resources and distribution systems. Large areas of agricultural land have been lost to premature subdivisions. Parallel to the subdivision of farmlands has been the extension of suburban growth on to the limestone hills to the north-west and north-east of Spanish Town. This has meant the installation of infrastructure in terrain requiring continuous energy inputs for the pumping of water supplies and has also created adverse impacts on the two aquifer recharge areas. In certain areas urban development has intruded into locations of high environmental value with consequent deleterious results on natural ecosystems. In addition, a large proportion of land originally zoned for manufacturing industry still stands vacant, or has been built on for alternative or illegal uses such as squatting.

The situation in most rapidly urbanising towns and cities in Jamaica has been one very similar to that found in the Kingston region. While most developments reflect the development standards and specifications of subdivisions, there are instances where developers have violated the standards or where land reserved for open space has been converted to other uses. Of primary concern in these rapidly urbanising towns, however, is the uncontrolled development which is encroaching onto land not designated for urban uses in the development order. In many rural parishes large tracts of good agricultural land have been converted into residential and commercial areas. It is also in these rural towns that a large percentage of land converted to urban land takes place in the informal sector and in some instances surpasses the conversion of land in the formal sector. Most of this informal conversion to urban land occurs on steep slopes zoned for conservation in the development order area or occurs in semi-rural areas found primarily on the periphery of the city outside of the development order boundary.

Infilling

Infilling in the city of Kingston has not been as a result of deliberate policy by planners, but rather as a result of the increasing scarcity of large tracts of land for development purposes. Infilling and intensification of land uses in the city is a policy that should be actively pursued. Currently infilling and intensification in the city takes place at two levels. First, infilling has been taking place on large single residential lots which have been redeveloped into apartment or townhouse developments. These developments are supported and promoted by the Town Planning Department. Infilling and intensification is also occurring illegally in the city of Kingston. In this instance, many older residential areas of the city are being converted to commercial and industrial land. These uses are illegal because the 1966 Kingston Development Order still applies and has zoned these areas for residential use. However, there is a need to recognise that the city must grow and we must plan for this growth. Mixed land uses is the only option that is feasible in such areas at this time and strategies and policies to channel growth must be developed and implemented.

Planned Development by the Government

Government agencies do develop land for urban use in Jamaica, but apart from the UDC they have not been a major force compared with the developmental activity of both the formal and informal components of the private sector. The UDC has been a major developer in the tourism sector in Montego Bay, Ocho Rios and Negril both in terms of a primary developer providing infrastructure and a secondary developer constructing commercial and residential buildings. Its land acquisition and development activities have had a major impact on the growth of Ocho Rios, and it still has plans for major new developments in Montego Bay and Negril. Since 1983, the UDC has been responsible for the CRTDP in more than eleven towns in Jamaica.

The UDC has extensive land holdings in the Kingston region, Montego Bay and other urban centres. However, whatever plans the UDC has to develop these lands is not generally known by the public or agencies such as the Town Planning Department and the local planning authority in which these lands are located. While the corporation has met its obligations under the Act and has submitted its plans to the parish councils, these plans have often not been implemented as originally intended. Uncertainty therefore arises over what the plans for land which it still owns are and whether the UDC plans to develop these lands itself or make them available for private development in the short-term. With regard to the CRTPD, there is no established mechanism for coordination with other agencies such as the Town Planning Department and the Planning Institute of Jamaica (PIOJ). It is critical that there should be some inter-agency review of how these towns and cities might become the focal points for integrating spatial strategies and economic development policy.

Planned Decentralisation and New Towns

Planned decentralisation as proposed by the planners did not materialise as envisaged. The Kingston Regional Plan proposed the expansion of the urbanised region to extend to the new towns at Hellshire Hills with some amount of development taking place at Dawkins Pond (Portmore). The major attractions for Hellshire were government ownership and poor quality agricultural land. Hellshire was to be a well-planned series of new towns, but its development has been scaled back for several reasons including the development of Portmore.

One of the major problems associated with the proposed development of Hellshire was its poor accessibility from Kingston. In order to overcome this problem the Portmore Land Development Corporation, a private body, proposed and constructed a causeway which linked the area near Dawkins Pond to Newport West. This area became the new town of Portmore. Portmore's transformation into a middle-income housing estate in order to help remedy the chronic middle-income housing shortage in the KMA has been phenomenal. But, at the same time, it has served to undermine the development of Hellshire. Unlike Hellshire, which was the subject of extensive planning by the UDC, Portmore was developed largely by private developers. The lack of basic services in Portmore led to the UDC being instructed by the government in 1977 to plan and implement, in collaboration with WIHCON, a programme for the construction of social facilities.

Planning in Greater Portmore (10,000 houses) was more extensive than in Portmore, largely as a result of intense pressure from the general public that the mistakes made in the development of Portmore should not be repeated in Greater Portmore. Portmore has not fulfilled, however, the requirements for a new town as it lacks employment opportunities and most residents must seek employment in Kingston.

Regional and National Impacts

Despite the preparation of two National Physical Plans, planners have had very little influence at national and regional levels. Neither of these plans has been implemented and the National Settlement Strategy has not been used as intended (as a guide to socio-economic development) so that urbanisation would proceed on a rational basis. The National Settlement Strategy has not been used to synthesise many of the other development policies and provide the basis for making certain planning decisions. This is basically due to the fact that national planning is seen as the purview of economic planning, and the role of settlements in local economic development is not seen as being in an inextricably interdependent relationship.

The growth of towns in Jamaica has been related to the provision of job opportunities. Towns which have experienced substantial expansion of their employment opportunities over the last two decades have experienced high rates of population growth. Since the 1970s, there have been notable shifts in the location pattern of jobs and population in Jamaica. Growth in employment has been in tourism, manufacturing and other services. Growth in the bauxite industry had a significant impact on the centres which directly served the industry, but its effects were felt to a lesser extent throughout the parish when compared with the tourist industry.

In the rural areas, declining agriculture and the lack of employment opportunities have resulted in the decline of smaller urban centres which play a functional role in the development of these areas. This has contributed to migration from the smaller centres to the major urban centres. While not great in absolute terms, migration has placed additional burdens on all urban services but in particular on land and related urban infrastructure. The main issue here is that most development orders were prepared more than thirty years ago and because of their static nature have not able to keep pace with population growth. As a result urban expansion is not being guided to areas most suited for development as land for this purpose is not being made available on a timely basis. Pressure is therefore put on environmentally sensitive areas such as hillsides, and areas zoned for uses such as industry and conservation are often occupied by squatters.

Without any specific policies towards regional development a large proportion of investment is spread throughout the country according to sector priorities set up by different agencies in charge of their implementation. These projects have a profound impact on spatial development but none of these projects are guided by quantitative targets for growth in different locations. In addition, very few of the projects establish links between the sectors of the regional economy, thus reducing the possibilities to increase the regional capacity to achieve a greater degree of self-sustained regional development.

The Future

Spatial planning has probably not had the impact expected since the appointment of a town planning adviser in 1947 and the introduction of the Town and Country Planning Act in 1957. The Act introduced the development order as the regulatory tool through which planning control would be exercised. However, zoning regulations and subdivision standards are largely ignored by a large section of the population who find these standards unaffordable. For the future more attention needs to be paid to the issue of standards in an effort to make more affordable serviced land available for development. The process must involve all the stakeholders in the housing delivery process including the local authorities, consumers, developers and the agencies to which development applications are made. All criteria used in the assessment process should be discussed and decisions taken on how these standards should be incorporated as part of a standards review process.

For the future also there is an urgent need for a review of the current laws and regulations as they apply to planning and their relevance to issues such as sustainable development, poverty alleviation and an efficient and functioning land market. It is also necessary to recognise the links between spatial strategies and economic development; economic policies can no longer ignore the location implications. Project implementation requires a more explicit consideration of the socio-economic and spatial impacts of projects at a regional level throughout the entire project development and implementation process.

Improving institutional coordination and increasing local government involvement in spatial planning and development must be a priority concern in the ensuing decade. A more integrated outlook of all development efforts taking place in a parish or region, in a particular sector or group of sectors, will have beneficial effects. Policies to support the developmental roles that small and intermediate settlements can play need coordinated action between sector ministries and local government. Since projects proposed and designed by specific sector agencies and ministries have important effects on the development of small and intermediate settlements, such policies must be coordinated within the overall context of a settlement strategy.

The Local Government Reform Programme offers the opportunity of decentralisation in decision making and greater coordination of development tasks at a local level. Local government must play an increasing role in coordinating the development at a local level so as to ensure the required interaction between projects during implementation. In addition, local government is in a much better position than central government for articulating local needs. The Town Planning Department must assist local government in this task.

When the Town and Country Planning Act was introduced in 1957 its basic goal was to promote orderly development through development control mechanisms. This concept of planning needs to be adjusted if planning is to remain relevant and become effective in dealing with the issues facing the country at this time. Planning in the twenty-first century in Jamaica cannot continue to focus primarily on the processing of development applications. There are so many issues which demand that planners become involved and planning take a lead role. In the coming decade a new vision of planning by planners is urgently required. Creative policies must be designed which will lead to sustainable development in urban areas. The newly established National Environmental and Planning Agency (NEPA) will need to bring about a shift which will see policies directed at enabling towns and cities to become more economically, environmentally and socially sustainable.

Bibliography

Adelatec, (1964), *Adelatec Program for the Development of Negril and Surrounding Areas, Jamaica, W.I.,* vol. I. Lima, Peru

Albers, G., (1995), *Explaining Demands on Planning* – A Review of Historical Parallels in Proceedings of the International Society of City and Regional Planners held in Prague, 4–10 September, 1994, IsoCaRP

Ashworth, W., (1954), *The Genesis of Modern Town Planning: A Study in Economic and Social History of the Nineteenth and Twentieth Centuries,* Routledge and Kegan Paul, London

Auty, Richard M., (1995), *Patterns of Development, Resources, Policy and Economic Growth,* Edward Arnold, London

Bahl, R. and Linn, J., (1992), *Urban Public Finance in Developing Countries,* Oxford University Press, Oxford

Banerjee, T. and Schenk, S., (1984), 'Lower Order Cities and National Urbanisation Policies: China and India in Kammeier', in *Equity with Growth? Planning Perspectives for Small Towns in Developing Countries, Asian Institute of Technology, Bangkok* edited by D. H. and Swan P. J.

Berry, B. J. L. and Horton, F. E., (1970), *Geographic Perspectives on Urban Systems,* Prentice-Hall, New Jersey

Bonnick, G., (1995), *Central Planning Unit to National Planning Agency,* in *Daily Gleaner,* Wednesday, 25 October and Thursday, 26 October 1995, Kingston, Jamaica

Branch, Melville C., (1998), *Comprehensive Planning for the 21st Century: General Theory and Principles,* Praeger, Westport, Connecticut

Central Housing and Planning Authority, Kingston, Jamaica, Annual Reports 1949 to 1953, 1953

Central Planning Unit (1957), *National Plan for Jamaica 1957–1967,* Government Printing Office, Kingston, Jamaica

Chadwick, G., (1971), *A Systems View of Planning,* Pergamon, Oxford

Chapin, F. S., (1965), *Urban Land Use Planning* (second edition), University of Illinois Press, Urbana

Cherry, G. E., (1972), *Urban Change and Planning: A History of Urban Development in Britain since 1750*, Foulis, Henley

Clarke, C. G., (1975), *Kingston, Jamaica: Urban Growth and Social Change 1692–1962*, University of California Press, Berkeley

Construction Resource and Development Centre, (1987) *Analysis of the Costs of Alternative Development Standards*, Report of the USAID Sponsored Town Planning Review Project, The Urban Institute, Washington, D.C.

Corbridge, S., (ed.) (1995), *Development Studies: A Reader*, Edward Arnold, London

Cox, J. and Cox, O., (1985), *Self Built and Expanded Housing in Jamaica: A Comparative Study of Single Storey Housing from 12 Projects*, Shankland/Cox, London

Cross, M., (1979), *Urbanisation and Urban Growth in the Caribbean*, Cambridge University Press, London

Cullingworth, J. B., (1988), *Town and Country Planning in Britain* (tenth edition), Unwin Hyman, London

Department of Housing, Kingston, Jamaica, Annual Report of the Department of Housing (mimeo), 1959

Department of Housing, Kingston, Jamaica, Annual Report of the Department of Housing (mimeo), 1961

Department of Housing, Kingston, Jamaica, First Report of the Committee on Middle Class Housing, 1954

Design Collaborative (1982) Development Plan UDC Designated Lands, Kingston, Jamaica

Dickenson, J. P., Clarke, C. G., Gould, W. T. S., Prothero, R. M., Siddle, D. J., Smith, C. T., Thomas-Hope, E. M. and Hodgkiss, A. G., (1991), *A Geography of the Third World*, Routledge, London

Dowall, D. E. and Clarke, G., (1991), *A Framework for Reforming Urban Land Policies in Developing Countries*, Urban Management Program, UNCHS, Nairobi, Kenya

Drakakis-Smith, D., (1987), *The Third World City*, Methuen, London

Dunham, D. M. and Hilhorst, J. G. M., (eds.) (1971), *Issues in Regional Planning: A Selection of Seminar Papers*, Mouton, The

Hague

Faludi, A., (1973), *Planning Theory*, Pergamon Press, Oxford

– (1978), *A Reader in Planning Theory*, Pergamon Press, London

Farvacque-Vitkovic, C. and Godin, L., (1988), *The Future of African Cities, Challenges and Priorities for Urban Development*, The World Bank, Washington D.C.

Farvacque, C. and McAuslan, P., (1991), *Reforming Urban Land Policies and Institutions in Developing Countries*, Urban Management Program, UNDP/World Bank/UNCHS, Nairobi, Kenya

Foley, D. L., (1973), 'British Town Planning: One Ideology or Three?' in *Planning Theory*, Faludi (ed.) Pergamon Press, London

Friedmann, J. and Alonso W. (eds.), (1964), *Regional Development Planning: A Reader*, The MIT Press, Cambridge

Friedmann, J. and Weaver C., (1979), *Territory and Function: The Evolution of Regional Planning*, Edward Arnold, London

Friedmann, J., (1992), *Empowerment: The Politics of Alternative Development*, Blackwell, Oxford

Gager, W., (1991), *The Greater Portmore Development – An Objective Assessment in BSAJ*, May 1991, Kingston, Jamaica

Glasson, J., (1974), *An Introduction to Regional Planning*, Hutchinson, London

Geddes P., (1968, orig. 1915), *Cities in Evolution: An Introduction to the Town Planning Movement and the Study of Civics*, Benn, London

George, V. and Warren C., (1984), 'The Changing Caribbean: The Kingston Waterfront: Evaluation of a Redevelopment Scheme', in *Caribbean Geography*, vol. 1, no. 3, Longman, Jamaica

George, V. and Wolffe C., (eds.) (1989), 'Proceedings of A Caribbean Regional Workshop on Development Standards' in *Development Standards for the Caribbean*, Town and Country Planning Association of Jamaica, Kingston, Jamaica

Gilbert, A., (ed.) (1976), *Development Planning and Spatial Structure*, John Wiley and Sons, London

Gilbert, A. and Gugler, J., (1992), *Cities, Poverty and Development: Urbanisation in the Third World* (second edition), Oxford

University Press, Oxford

Grossman, F., Hayes, O. R., Miller, K. L. and Data Resources International Ltd., (1994), *Financing Improved Services and Infrastructure for Downtown Kingston*, (mimeo) prepared for USAID Regional Housing and Urban Development for the Caribbean, Washington D.C.

Gulger, J., (ed.) (1996), *The Urban Transformation of the Developing World*, Oxford University Press, New York

Hall, P., (1970), *The Theory and Practice of Regional Planning*, Pemberton, London

– (1988), *Cities of Tomorrow: An Intellectual History of Urban Planning and Design in the Twentieth Century*, Blackwell, Oxford

– (1992), *Urban and Regional Planning* (third edition), Routledge, London.

Hall, P., Gracey, H., Drewett, R. and Thomas R., (1973) *The Containment of Urban England*, 2 vols., Allen & Unwin, London

Hall, P. and Pfeiffer, U., (2000), *Urban Future 21 – A Global Agenda for Twenty-First Cities*, F&FN Spon, London

Hardy, D., (1991), *From Garden Cities to New Towns: Campaigning for Town and Country Planning 1899–1946*, F&FN Spon, London

Heap, D., (1991), *An Outline of Planning Law*, Sweet & Maxwell, London

Hilhorst, J. G. M., (1971), *Regional Planning: A Systems Approach*, Rotterdam University Press, Rotterdam

Hill, S., (1983), *An Analysis of the Applications for Commercial Space along the Kingston Waterfront*, (mimeo), Urban Development Corporation, Kingston, Jamaica

Howard, E., (1965), *Garden Cities of Tomorrow* (with preface by Osborn F. J.), Faber, London

Hudson, B. J., (1980), 'Urbanisation and Planning in the West Indies', in *Caribbean Quarterly* vol. 26, no. 3, September 1980, Kingston, Jamaica

IDB Projects (1999) vol. VI, Issue no. 8, Inter-American Development Bank, Washington D.C.

Journal of Development Studies, (1993), *Beyond Urban Bias*, Special Issue, vol. 29.

Kammeier, D. H. and Swan P., (eds.) (1984), *Equity with Growth?*

Planning Perspectives for Small Towns in Developing Countries, Asian Institute of Technology, Bangkok

King, A., (1990), *Urbanism, Colonialism and the World Economy*, Routledge, London

Knight G., (1974), Investment Decision Implementation Case Study: Kingston Waterfront Redevelopment Project in Symposium on Urban Development, National Housing Bank, Rio de Janeiro

Kingsley, G. T. and McLean, P., (1987), *Land Use and Development Pressures in the Kingston Metropolitan Area*, Report of the USAID Sponsored Town Planning Review Project, (mimeo), The Urban Institute, Washington, D.C.

Kingsley, G. T. and Wines S. W., (1987), *Town Planning and Land Development in Jamaica: An Agenda for Reform*, Final Phase I Report of the USAID Sponsored Town Planning Review Project, (mimeo), The Urban Institute, Washington, D.C.

Kingsley, G. T., Olsen, P. and Telgarsky, J. P., (1989), *Improving Jamaica's Land Regulations and Processing Systems*, Final Phase II Report of the USAID Sponsored Town Planning Review Project, (mimeo), The Urban Institute, Washington, D.C.

Kingsley, G. T., (1990), 'The Urban-Economic Nexus in Caribbean Development', in *Proceedings of Conference on Urban Management*, held Sept., 5 to 7, 1990, Bridgetown, Barbados

Ling, A., (ed.) (1978), *Urban and Regional Planning and Development in the Commonwealth*, Howell Publications, Cambridgeshire

Matalon, J., (1996), 'The Matalon Experience in Housing Development in Affordable Housing', in *Proceedings of the National Housing Trust's 20th Anniversary Housing Symposium*, Francis, A., George, V. and Smith, M., (eds.) (1996) National Housing Trust, Kingston Jamaica

Matalon, J., 'Ten Thousand Houses', in *The Builder*, vol. 2, no. 2, May 1990, Kingston, Jamaica

McCray-Goldsmith, J. and Mohammed, A., (1994), *Operation Pride: Draft Policy and Programmatic Framework*, prepared for the Office of the Prime Minister with support from USAID/RHUDO-CAR, (mimeo), Kingston, Jamaica

McHardy, P., (1994), *Improving the Process for Building and Development Applications at the Local Authority Level*, (mimeo), prepared for the Ministry of Local Government Reform Program, Ministry of Local Government, Kingston, Jamaica

– (1997a), *Jamaica's Settlement Strategy: A Review of Experiences and Potentials*, (mimeo), prepared for the Town Planning Department, Kingston, Jamaica

– (1997b), *National Resettlement Policy for Jamaica*, (mimeo), prepared for the World Bank and the Ministry of Environment and Housing, Kingston, Jamaica

– (1997c), *The Land Development Process: Improving the Regulatory Framework*, (mimeo), prepared for the Local Government Reform Programme Seminar on the Land Development Process, August 1997, Jamaica Conference Centre, Kingston, Jamaica

– (1997d), *Housing Provision and Policy Making in Jamaica: Charting the Level of Involvement of the Architect*, (mimeo), prepared for the Jamaica Institute of Architects for presentation at the Commonwealth Association of Architects Meeting, Goa, India 1997, Kingston, Jamaica

– (1997), *Revising Development Standards in Jamaica*, (mimeo), prepared for Intermediate Technology Group Enabling Housing Standards and Procedures Project, Rugby, UK

– (1999), *Comparative Analysis of Parish Baseline Circumstances Report*, (mimeo), prepared for CIDA's Jamaica: Supporting Local Government Reform Project, Kingston, Jamaica

McKay, L., (1987), 'Tourism and Changing Attitudes to Land in Negril', in *Land and Development in the Caribbean*, Besson, J. and Momsen, J., (eds.) (1987), Warwick University Caribbean Studies, Macmillan, London

McLoughlin, J. B., (1970), *Urban and Regional Planning*, Faber, London

Meyer, D., (1986), 'System of City Dynamics in Newly Industrializing Nations', in *Studies in Comparative International Development*

Miller, K. L., (1996), *Historical and Contemporary Perspectives on Local Government Reform in Jamaica* (mimeo), Ministry of Local Government Reform Program, ministry of local government, Kingston, Jamaica

Mills, G E., (1995), *Planning in Jamaica – The Early Years*, in PIOJ

40th Anniversary Supplement, *Daily Gleaner*, Wednesday, 25 October, 1995, Kingston, Jamaica

Ministry of Local Government, Kingston, Jamaica, Local Government Reform Program Ministry Paper 8/93 (mimeo), 1993

Mumford, L., (1938), *The Culture of Cities*, Brace and Co., Harcourt

Nettleford, R., (ed.) (1971), *Norman Washington Manley and the New Jamaica, Port of Spain and Kingston*, Longman, Caribbean.

Norton, A., (1978), *Shanties and Skyscrapers: Growth and Structure of Modern Kingston*, Institute of Social and Economic Research, University of the West Indies, Mona, Jamaica

NPA (National Planning Agency), (1978), *Urban Growth and Management Study Final Report*, Kingston, Jamaica

NPA (National Planning Agency), (1978), *The Hellshire Bay New Town: An Evaluation*, (mimeo), Kingston, Jamaica

NPA (National Planning Agency), (1972), *Regional Planning: A Strategy for Balanced Development with Special Reference to Jamaica*, (mimeo), Kingston, Jamaica

Odum, H. W. and Jocher, K., (eds.) (1945), *In Search of Regional Balance in America*, University of North Carolina Press, Chapel Hill

Office of the Prime Minister /ASCEND, Kingston, Jamaica, *Starter Standards Manual* (mimeo), 1996

Onibokun, A., (1990) Poverty as a Constraint on Citizen Participation in Urban Redevelopment in Developing Countries, *Urban Studies* 27, 371–384

PIOJ (Planning Institute of Jamaica), (1990), *Jamaica Five Year Development Plan 1990–1995*, Stephensons Litho, Kingston, Jamaica

Portes, A., Dore-Cabral, C. and Landolt, P., (eds.) (1997), *The Urban Caribbean: Transition to the New Global Economy*, John Hopkins University Press, Baltimore

Portes, A., Itzigsohn, J. and Dore-Cabral, C., (1997), 'Urbanisation in the Caribbean Basin: Social Change during the Years of the Crisis in Portes', in *The Urban Caribbean: Transition to the New Global Economy*, Dore-Cabral, C. and Landolt, P., (eds.) (1997), John Hopkins University Press,

Baltimore

Potter, R. B., (ed.) (1984), *Low Income Housing in the Developing World*, John Wiley and Sons, New York

Potter, R. B., (1985), *Urbanisation and Planning in the Third World*, St Martin's Press, New York

Potter, R. B., (ed.) (1989), *Urbanisation, Planning and Development in the Caribbean*, Mansell Press, London

Potter, R. B., (1992), *Urbanisation in the Third World*, Oxford University Press, Oxford

Potter, R. B. and Conway, D., (eds.) (1997), *Self Help Housing, the Poor, and the State in the Caribbean*, University of Tennessee Press, Knoxville

Ranson, P., (1985), *New Kingston: A Background Report*, (mimeo) Town Planning Department, Kingston, Jamaica

Reid, I., (1996), 'Financial Reform: Changing Relationships' in *Reform Outlook*, no. 3, May 1996, Local Government Reform Unit, Jamaica

Richardson, H. W., (1969), *Regional Economics: Location Theory, Urban Structure and Regional Change*, Praeger, New York

Richardson, H. W., (1982), Policies for Strengthening Small Cities in Developing Countries in Mathur, O. P. (ed.) *Small Cities and National Development*, UN Centre for Regional Development, Nagoya

Roberts, M., (1977), *An Introduction to Town Planning Techniques*, Hutchinson and Company Ltd., London

Rondinelli, D. A., (1975), *Urban and Regional Development Planning: Policy and Administration*, Cornell University Press, Ithaca

Rondinelli, D. A. and Ruddle, K., (1976), *Urban Functions in Rural Development: An Analysis of Integrated Spatial Development Policy*, (mimeo), Office of Urban Development, Technical Assistance Bureau, AID, Washington, D.C.

Rondinelli, D. A., (1983), *Secondary Cities in Developing Countries: Policies for Diffusing Urbanisation*, Sage, London

Rodwin, L., (ed.) (1987), *Shelter, Settlement and Development*, Allen & Unwin, Boston

Shankland & Cox Overseas, (1971), *A Report on Montego Bay*, prepared for the UDC, Shankland & Cox, Kingston, Jamaica

Shankland & Cox Overseas, (1969), *Ocho Rios: An Analysis of*

Development Potential, Shankland & Cox, Kingston, Jamaica

Shankland & Cox, (1971), *Low Cost Housing in Jamaica: Study and Proposals for the Redevelopment of a Squatter Area in Trench Town Kingston*, Shankland & Cox, Kingston, Jamaica

Sharma, K. L., (1984), 'Rural-Urban Integration in National Development: S Strategy of Spatial Planning for Human Settlements in Kenya', in *Equity with Growth? Planning Perspectives for Small Towns in Developing Countries*, Kammeier, H. D. and Swan, P., (eds.) Asian Institute of Technology, Bangkok

Smith, D. A., (1996), *Third World Cities in Global Perspective*, Westview, Boulder, Colorado

STATIN (Statistical Institute of Jamaica) *Population Census 1991 Parish of Kingston, vol. 1, Part 1*, Printing Unit STATIN, Kingston, Jamaica, 1995

STATIN (Statistical Institute of Jamaica) *Population Census 1991, Parish of St Andrew, vol. 1, Part 2*, Printing Unit STATIN, Kingston, Jamaica, 1995

STATIN (Statistical Institute of Jamaica) *Population Census 1991, Parish of St Thomas, vol. 1, Part 3*, Printing Unit STATIN, Kingston, Jamaica, 1995

STATIN (Statistical Institute of Jamaica) *Population Census 1991, Parish of Portland, vol. 1, Part 4*, Printing Unit STATIN, Kingston, Jamaica, 1995

STATIN (Statistical Institute of Jamaica) *Population Census 1991, Parish of St Mary, vol. 1, Part 5*, Printing Unit STATIN, Kingston, Jamaica, 1995

STATIN (Statistical Institute of Jamaica) *Population Census 1991, Parish of St Ann, vol. 1, Part 6*, Printing Unit STATIN, Kingston, Jamaica, 1995

STATIN (Statistical Institute of Jamaica) *Population Census 1991, Parish of Trelawny, vol. 1, Part 7*, Printing Unit STATIN, Kingston, Jamaica, 1995

STATIN (Statistical Institute of Jamaica) *Population Census 1991, Parish of St James, vol. 1, Part 8*, Printing Unit STATIN, Kingston, Jamaica, 1995

STATIN (Statistical Institute of Jamaica) *Population Census 1991, Parish of Hanover, vol. 1, Part 9*, Printing Unit STATIN,

Kingston, Jamaica. 1995

STATIN (Statistical Institute of Jamaica) *Population Census 1991, Parish of Westmoreland, vol. 1, Part 10,* Printing Unit STATIN, Kingston, Jamaica, 1995

STATIN (Statistical Institute of Jamaica) *Population Census 1991, Parish of St Elizabeth, vol. 1, Part 11,* Printing Unit STATIN, Kingston, Jamaica, 1995

STATIN (Statistical Institute of Jamaica) *Population Census 1991, Parish of Manchester, vol. 1, Part 12,* Printing Unit STATIN, Kingston, Jamaica, 1995

STATIN (Statistical Institute of Jamaica) *Population Census 1991, Parish of Clarendon, vol. 1, Part 13,* Printing Unit STATIN, Kingston, Jamaica, 1995

STATIN (Statistical Institute of Jamaica) *Population Census 1991, Parish of St Catherine, vol. 1, Part 14,* Printing Unit STATIN, Kingston, Jamaica, 1995

Taylor, J. L. and Williams, D. G., (eds.) (1982), *Urban Planning Practice in Developing Countries*, Pergamon Press, New York

Town Planning Division, Ministry of Mining and Natural Resources, (1973), *A Manual for Development*, prepared by UNDP, Advisory Planning Committee and Town and Country Planning Authority, A1 Printers, Kingston, Jamaica

Town Planning Department, Ministry of Finance and Planning, (1982), *A Manual for Development*, United Cooperative Printers, Kingston, Jamaica

Town Planning Department, Ministry of the Public Service, (1993), *A Manual for Development*, (mimeo), TPD, Kingston, Jamaica

Town Planning Department, Ministry of the Public Service, (1992), *Proposal for the Introduction of Minimum Standards for Housing Development and Upgrading in Low Income Areas in Jamaica*, (mimeo), TPD, Kingston, Jamaica

Town Planning Department, Ministry of Finance and Planning, (1971), *A National Physical Plan for Jamaica 1970 to 1990*, Kingston, Jamaica

Town Planning Department, Ministry of Mining and Natural Resources, (1978), *A National Physical Plan for Jamaica 1978 to 1998*, Government Printing Office, Kingston, Jamaica

Town Planning Department, Government Printing Office, Kingston, Jamaica, The Town and Country Planning (St Catherine Coast) Provisional Development Order 1964, 1964

Town Planning Department, Government Printing Office, Kingston, Jamaica, The Town and Country Planning (Kingston) Development Order 1966, 1966

Town Planning Department, Government Printing Office, Kingston, Jamaica, The Town and Country Planning (Negril Green Island) Provisional Development Order 1958, 1958

Town Planning Department, Government Printing Office, Kingston, Jamaica, The Town and Country Planning (Negril Green Island) Provisional Development Order 1981, 1981

Town Planning Department, Jamaica Printing Services (1992) Ltd., Government Printers, Kingston, Jamaica, The Town and Country Planning (St Ann Parish) Provisional Development Order 1998, 1988

Town Planning Department, Ministry of Mining and Natural Resources, (1972), *North Coast Regional Development Plan*, Jamaican UN Special Fund Project 'Assistance in Physical Planning', Kingston, Jamaica

Town and Country Planning Association of Jamaica, (1986), *Spatial Implications of Economic Policy*, Proceedings of a seminar, TCPAJ, Kingston, Jamaica

Turner, R., (ed.) (1993), *Sustainable Environmental Economics and Management*, Belhaven, London

UNCHS, Nairobi, Kenya, *The Role of Small and Intermediate Settlements in National Development*, 1985

UNDP (1973) *Assistance in Physical Development Planning: The Kingston Regional Plan*, technical report prepared for the Government of Jamaica, UN, New York

USAID, (1985), *Secondary Towns: An Overview of Five Case Studies*, USAID, Washington D.C.

Urban Development Corporation, Kingston, Jamaica, CRTDP – *Phase 1, Ex-post Evaluation* (mimeo), 1992

Urban Development Corporation, Kingston, Jamaica, *Cortowns* (mimeo), 1971

Urban Development Corporation, Kingston, Jamaica, *Ocho Rios Impact Study 1986/87*, 1988

Urban Development Corporation, Kingston, Jamaica, *Montego Bay Waterfront (Explanatory Notes)* (mimeo), 1984

Urban Development Corporation, *Planning and Implementation of Urban Development with Special Emphasis on the Jamaican Experience*, 1979

Urban Development Corporation, Kingston, Jamaica, *Hellshire Bay Hellshire Park Estate – Southern Sector: Phase I* (mimeo), 1977

Urban Development Corporation, Kingston, Jamaica, UDC Seminar 14–18 July 1975 (mimeo), 1975

Urban Development Corporation, Kingston, Jamaica, Hellshire Bay Draft Town Plan (mimeo), 1970

Urban Growth and Management Study, Final Report, National Planning Agency, November 1978, Kingston, Jamaica

Vance, J. E., (1990), *Urban Morphology in Western Civilization*, John Hopkins University Press, Baltimore

Ward, S. V., (1994), *Planning and Urban Change*, Paul Chapman Publishing Ltd., London

Wason, A. T., (1984), Workshop Report on Inspection Procedures and Enforcement Regulations, Kingston, Jamaica, 3 July 1984, Office of Disaster Preparedness and Emergency Relief, Jamaica in association with the Pan-Caribbean Disaster Preparedness and Prevention Project

World Bank, Cities in Transition – World Bank Urban and Local Government Strategy, (2000), The World Bank Infrastructure Group, Washington D.C.

INDEX

Search for...
Shankland & cox
P. 88 - manual for housing etc.

26/06 ~~what~~ unclear application process for
subdivisions
— does it go to Mandeville for water?
& the time period. ~~etc~~

. a virgin of development
→ Jamaica
— Not with father all the time.

Some stay, some go...
— who stays? only those who
don't want to work hard?
— does it need opportunity? or
just hard work?

9 781844 260195